Sue Smith

REVIEWING T

REVIEWING
Reviews

a woman's place on the book page

written and edited by

Women in Publishing

Margaret Cooter
Katharine Harding
Lesley Levene
Sally MacEachern
Shân Morley Jones
Ros Schwartz
Jane Tarlo
Ann Treneman

Journeyman

First published in Great Britain by the Journeyman Press

The Journeyman Press Ltd, 97 Ferme Park Road, Crouch End, London N8 9SA

Designed by Graphic Detail (01) 520 5029

First edition 1987

87 88 89 5 4 3 2 1

Printed by Robert Hartnoll (1985) Ltd, Bodmin

British Library Cataloguing in Publication Data

Reviewing the reviews : a woman's place on
  the book page.
  1. Sexism in book reviewing 2. English
  literature — Women authors — History
  and criticism
  I. Women in Publishing *(Organisation)*
  820.9'9287   PN98.B7

  ISBN 1-85172-007-3

Acknowledgements

We would like to thank all the members of Women in Publishing who supported us both financially and morally; Marie King, Jan Schubert and Jill Maskens, who lightened the burden of research; Talia Rogers for her constructive reading of the finished manuscript; Barbara James for valuable insights; Sarah Beal for her assistance; Annie McLean for use of her computer; the four authors who so generously gave us their time: Barbara Burford, Andrea Dworkin, Zoë Fairbairns and Margaret Forster; Dale Spender for her support; and Moving Lines Ltd, who provided a comfortable venue for many of our meetings. Thanks also to P. Payne and N. Galwey for statistical advice; and to the Library Association Library, the London College of Printing Library, and the Fawcett Library for help with sources and background materials.

Contents

List of Charts

Introduction

In the 19th century, a number of women writers resorted to using male pseudonyms, and no wonder when they received reviews such as this one of George Eliot's work when it was revealed she was a woman:

> 'There is a good deal of coarseness, which it is unpleasant to think of as the work of a woman, and, as we shall have occasion to observe more fully hereafter, the influence which these novels are likely to exercise over public taste is not altogether such as a woman should aim at.'

And yet, when she was believed to be a man, she had been described as 'a gentleman of high church tendencies'.

This was over a century ago. What about women writers now; do they enjoy unbiased treatment on the book review pages?

Over the last decade there has been a 'trend' for women's books. It started with women's publishing houses like Virago, The Women's Press and Sheba, which mainstream publishers were sceptical of at first, but now too have jumped on the bandwagon and created women writers series. The book trade has obviously realised that there is money to be made out of women's writing. But there is a discrepancy between the apparent interest in women's books and the actual notice they receive in the press. A casual glance at the book pages will often show a much larger number of reviews of books by male authors, but so far there has been no in-depth study of the treatment of women authors on the book review pages.

The issue of women's books and book reviews was the subject of a meeting of Women in Publishing in June 1985. It became clear that although many of us were aware that women's books appeared to receive less attention on the book pages, there was a dearth of concrete information on the subject. A group of eight women present at that meeting decided to investigate further and carry out a systematic survey over a period of one year to find out whether there was bias and, if so, to what extent.

We set out to establish what percentage of women authors were reviewed in comparison to men. To do this, we monitored 28 publications - weeklies, monthlies, newspapers, general magazines and literary reviews - for the year 1985. As our research progressed, we realised that it was not just a question of counting the number of men and women authors reviewed in a particular issue. Other considerations, such as positioning on the page and the amount of space devoted to a review, needed to be looked at when evaluating the overall balance between men and women authors.

In our survey, we looked at the following questions:

- How does the space devoted to women's books compare to that devoted to men's?
- Where are reviews of women's books placed on the page?
- Are women reviewers confined mainly to fiction?
- Are there fewer female reviewers?
- Do reviews influence book buyers and librarians, or help to sell books?

As well as analysing the publications, we interviewed the editors of the book pages to find out how they allocated books for review, whether they had any particular policy on reviewing, and what guidelines (if any) they issued to reviewers. We have tried to unravel the mysterious process by which certain books find their way on to the review pages while the vast majority do not. We talked to 25 publishers - mainstream, feminist, paperback and hardback - to find out how they went about targeting review copies of books and whether books by women authors were channelled towards particular publications. As for the booksellers and librarians, to what extent are they influenced by reviews? We asked a number of them whether readers' requests reflected the recommendations of book reviewers. And last, but not least, we talked to the people without whom there would be no books at all - the authors. How do they feel about their treatment by the reviewers? Margaret Forster, Barbara Burford, Andrea Dworkin and Zoë

Fairbairns describe their experiences in the claws of the critics.

The following excerpt illustrates the criteria some male reviewers apply when reviewing books by women:

> 'From the photograph supplied of Mss Casey Miller and Kate Swift, I should judge that neither was sexually very attractive . . . A sense of grievance can often bring out the worst in people, and there is no reason to extend our sympathy where the motives of these disgruntled feminist agitators is simply to make a nuisance of themselves. This would appear to be the inspiration behind Swift and Miller's *Handbook of Non-Sexist Writing*.'[2]

This kind of reviewing shows that the relative number of reviews of books by women and the amount of space given to them are not the only areas where bias may exist. It can also be detected in the tone of the reviews, such reviews being printed for 'entertainment value' rather than as an academic appraisal of a serious work. Although we appreciate that book reviews have to make good reading, we wonder whether anyone would describe a book by a male author by making disparaging comments about his appearance rather than discussing the contents of his book? In writing this kind of review, the male reviewer remains centre stage and the book itself becomes almost irrelevant. We have not examined the tone of the reviews in detail in this survey as we have limited ourselves to the measurable criteria such as length and positioning on the page. But it is another element we became increasingly aware of during our study.

In 1985, an average of 1,000 books a week were published in Great Britain. *The Times Literary Supplement*, which is almost entirely devoted to book reviews, assessed only 3,000 titles that year, so it becomes obvious that book review pages are highly selective. Similarly, we had to be selective in this survey as it was not possible to monitor every single publication. We have aimed for a balance by analysing publications entirely devoted to book reviews, such as *The Times Literary Supplement*, as well as general newspapers, socialist publications, such as *Marxism Today*, general magazines and women's magazines, both feminist and mass market.

Our book is divided into two sections. In Part One, written by Ann Treneman, we set out the results of our monitoring of 28 publications, presenting the facts and stats. In Part Two, we take a closer look at the processes operating behind the scenes and expand on the evidence revealed in Part One with comment and opinion from the people involved in steering the books towards the book pages - the publishers and literary editors - and from those influenced by the reviews - the booksellers and librarians.

Part One

Methodology

The main book pages of 28 publications were studied in this survey. The list was compiled to reflect variety, both in the aim of a publication and its form. (For listing, see Chart 1.) Twelve issues from each publication in 1985 were surveyed. This means that for monthly publications all issues for the year were examined, while for weeklies, dailies and semi-monthlies the first week of each month was surveyed. The only exception is the monthly magazine *Woman and Home*, for which 11 issues were surveyed.[1] All issues were examined for the quarterly *School Librarian*, the bi-monthly *Fiction Magazine* and *New Socialist*, which put out a combined July/August issue. (For *School Librarian*, the figures are based on reviews featured in the section for the 11-15 age group.)

For each book review, the following factors were noted: the title of the book and the author's name; the sex of the author (or, if applicable, editor); the book's publisher; whether it was fiction or non-fiction; the sex of the reviewer; the width and length of the review; and its position on the page. (The research form is shown in the Appendix.) When the sex of an author or reviewer could not be determined, as in cases where initials were used and the review gave no clue as to the sex of the author either, the sex was listed as 'unknown'. Books written or edited jointly by a man and a woman or by a group were also classified as 'unknown'. The review width was measured to one-sixteenth of an inch while its length was measured to one-fourth of an inch. From these figures, all reviews could be computed into square inches.

The statistics were then compiled for monthly and yearly totals. The latter are used in the charts appearing in Part One. In most charts, the publications are listed according to statistical results. In some cases, however, they are analysed by category. The categories - literary, education, socialist, women's, general readership news-

Methodology

	circulation*	type of publica- tion†	no. of issues surveyed	no. of reviews seen
LITERARY				
Fiction Magazine	-	b	6	39
Literary Review	7,000[1]	m	12	436
London Review of Books	15,000	f	12	350
The Times Literary Supplement	28,833[2]	w	12	650
EDUCATION				
School Librarian	5,000[3]	q	4	138
The Times Higher Education Supplement	15,285[2]	w	12	325
NEWSPAPERS				
Daily Telegraph	1,156,304[4]	d	12	266
Financial Times	251,554[4]	d	12	135
Guardian	524,264[4]	d	12	197
Mail on Sunday	1,616,860[4]	w	12	28
Observer	778,207[4]	w	12	453
Sunday Times	1,149,116[4]	w	12	293
The Times	471,483[4]	d	12	160
GENERAL				
City Limits	27,415[2]	w	12	127
Listener	33,277[2]	w	12	140
New Society	23,013[5]	w	12	135
New Statesman	28,375[2]	w	12	171
Punch	65,041[6]	w	12	66
Spectator	25,636[4]	w	12	107
SOCIALIST				
Marxism Today	7,500	m	12	73
New Socialist	24,232[5]	m	11	53
WOMEN'S				
Company	207,860[2]	m	12	76
Cosmopolitan	391,533[2]	m	12	76
Good Housekeeping	351,655[2]	m	12	64
Options	225,974[2]	m	12	112
She	210,935[2]	m	12	162
Spare Rib	30,000	m	12	63
Woman and Home	568,938[2]	m	11	93

*Figures taken from Benn's Directory
† q: quarterly; b: bi-monthly; m: monthly;
  f: fortnightly; w: weekly; d: daily
1 given at 12,000 in Willings Press Guide 1986
2 ABC figures for July-December 1985

3 given as 4,500 in Willings Press Guide 1986
4 ABC figures Jan-June 1986
5 ABC figures Jan-June 1984
6 ABC figures Jan-June 1985

paper and general readership magazine - reflect either the form of a publication or its aim. The categories were allotted on the most general terms in order still to allow for diversity within each area. For instance, some of the women's magazines could have been categorised as feminist. But rather than create a feminist category (and then have to define exactly what a 'feminist' publication would be), we chose to group them all as women's publications. This is also true of the general magazine category in terms of socialism. Some of the publications may be viewed as socialist, but we chose only those that examined socialism as their main aim to occupy the socialist category.

Ann Treneman

❛In   Newstatesmanning, the critic must always be on top of, or better than, the person criticised.❜

Stephen Potter

I. The Literary Dinner Party

The potential guests arrive ... well prepared for what is to be their Judgement Day. Each comes complete with an 'introduction' - a praise-filled blurb designed to make each stand out as an exceptional candidate. Groomed carefully for the occasion, their appearances have been tailored to attract, intrigue and arouse the curiosity. For these guests are new books and the invitation they are all seeking is to be included on that exclusive list of titles bound for the book review pages. They are on parade before the literary editors, who must sift through the masses of brown-paper-wrapped parcels with a discriminating eye. But while this selection process may be a private one, the results are very public indeed. Any reader need only turn to the book review pages to see, spelled out in black and white, the current 'Who's Who in Books' for that week or month.

But who is who on the books pages? And how do women authors fare in this contest for invitations? The answer, culled from our examination of 5,018 reviews, is twofold: she is either a coveted guest or something of a wallflower. For the guests of the book review pages are hardly akin to those at your average dinner party. Balancing the sexes may be seen as necessary for affable dinner chit-chat, but such a mixture is rarely found in the invitation lists of the 28 publications studied.

Out of those 28, it is in the women's magazines, and the women's magazines only, that the female author is the star turn. On the review pages of these seven publications, the spotlight is turned on her. Outside of this women's realm, however, the glare of publicity diminishes sharply. In all the other 21 publications, she is left in the shadows while the male author takes centre stage.

This split holds true regardless of the type of publication or its particular politics or purpose. The results may not seem especially surprising for women's magazines, which after all are created for and mostly by women. There is, however, a world of difference between such publications as *Woman and Home*, *Spare Rib* and *Cosmopolitan*. But while those differences may be reflected in the content of the book reviews themselves, the survey shows that all agree on the favourite sex of author on those pages. The diversity in the other 21 publications is even greater. Just about the only thing they all may seem to have in common is that they are not specifically geared to male or female readers. But the results of this survey show they also share a clear preference for the male author. For whether they are to the left or right of the political spectrum, a quality Sunday newspaper or a literary magazine, devoted to humour or education, their book sections are concerned mainly with reviewing books by men. They may be aimed for a general (i.e. mixed sex) readership, but to some extent all of the 21 could be called 'men's' publications.

This isn't to say that there aren't various degrees of preference. A look at Chart 2 reveals the percentages for each publication, and it shows that the tilt towards a favourite sex of author varies from the relatively slight to the precarious. There are extremes at both ends of the spectrum: the feminist monthly *Spare Rib* reviews almost solely books by women, while the review pages of the *Spectator* are overwhelmingly devoted to male authors. Of the 28, the most balanced were *Woman and Home* and *School Librarian*. Their relatively slight tilt means that these two publications, plus *She* magazine, were the only ones in the survey where the results for favourite sex of author are not necessarily definitive: that is, the figures are so close that in these three cases the 'unknown' books, if they could have been categorised by sex, were theoretically capable of tilting the balance the other way.

The statistics also show that the preference for a favourite author is less marked in the women's magazines. Excluding *Spare Rib*, the lowest percentage of male authors found in the remaining six women's magazines was *Cosmopolitan* at almost 30 per cent. On the other hand, the percentage of women authors in the other 21 publications was lower than 30 per cent in 17 cases. On the book review pages, most general readership publications are clearly more male-oriented than women's magazines are female-oriented.

But does this male slant in general readership publications

■ CHART 2 ■

WHO'S GETTING REVIEWED?

	percentage of books by		
	females	males	unknown
Spare Rib	98.41	1.59	0
Cosmopolitan	67.11	28.95	3.95
Company	64.47	31.58	3.95
Options	57.89	35.09	7.02
Good Housekeeping	57.81	32.81	9.38
She	48.15	39.51	12.35
Woman and Home	45.16	36.56	18.28
School Librarian	38.41	47.83	13.77
City Limits	37.01	62.20	0.79
Fiction Magazine	35.90	64.10	0
Listener	29.22	66.88	3.90
Literary Review	28.90	64.45	6.65
New Statesman	27.49	65.50	7.02
Daily Telegraph	27.17	65.94	6.88
The Times	26.25	68.75	5.00
Punch	21.21	74.24	4.55
New Socialist	20.75	73.58	5.66
Sunday Times	19.80	68.94	11.26
Observer	19.47	74.62	5.91
The Times Literary Supplement	19.38	77.54	3.08
Marxism Today	19.18	64.38	16.44
New Society	18.52	74.07	7.41
Guardian	17.77	75.13	7.11
Spectator	17.76	82.24	0
London Review of Books	16.57	78.00	5.43
Financial Times	15.56	77.78	6.67
Mail on Sunday	14.58	79.17	6.25
The Times Higher Education Supplement	9.54	72.92	17.54

merely reflect a world in which women publish or have published fewer books, or does it point up a pervasive sexism in how books are chosen for review? Because of the lack of information on books published, it's a simple question that is difficult to even begin to answer. In 1985, 52,994 books were published in Great Britain, but there are no statistics available on how many of those were by men and women. While the general statistic given for the average percentage of women-authored books is 20 per cent, we wanted to try and check that for the year 1985.[1]

To do this, a representative sampling was done of the *British National Bibliography*, a comprehensive listing of published books, for 1985.[2] This survey showed that about 18 per cent of the books were written by women and 51 per cent by men. (The remainder were unknown, mixed or group authors.) This average was further broken down into two categories - general books that you would expect to find in a reasonably stocked bookshop and specialist books that were academic. In this breakdown, women wrote 25 per cent of general books and 5 per cent of specialist books.

While these figures are valuable in themselves, they do not shed particular light on the question of whether women authors are discriminated against in the books chosen for review. This is because it isn't known just how many of the books written by men or women end up vying for review on the literary editor's desk. For instance, the figure on specialist books could indicate that there might be a good reason that *The Times Higher Education Supplement* features women authors less than 10 per cent of the time. But such an indicator may be faulty: it could be the case that women wrote, say, 20 per cent of the books sent to the *THES*.

But while it is not possible to draw any conclusions on whether sexism is behind the lack of women authors featured on the pages of the 'men's' publications, it is possible to examine the question of discrimination in another way. Once books have been chosen for review, how are they treated on the books page? Are women's books treated roughly the same as those by men? For if all books are not created equal in the first place, those inequalities can be enhanced in how they are reviewed. The placement and the length of a review signal to the reader the relative importance of a given book. In this way, the books page communicates much more than just the reviewers' opinions. Its composition is a reflection of the literary universe, as seen by that particular publication, and its messages about that world, although coded, cannot help but be absorbed.

The first aspect we examined was that of length, and the percentages in Chart 3 show how much space in each publication was given over to reviews of women's and men's books. The results tend to mirror the percentages of women and male authors that were given in Chart 2 with one important difference: in most cases the percentage of space given the favourite sex of author is higher. This increase means that women's magazines, in general, give books by women authors longer reviews than those by men; in most of the other 21 publications, longer reviews are given to books by men. And so, in terms of length of review, the general trend is that the favourite sex of author is confirmed in his/her position of authority.

What this means for women authors is that, if they get reviewed at all in the general readership publications, they can expect to receive a shorter review than their male colleague for no apparent reason other than the fact they happen to be female. On the women's magazines, the same thing is true for male authors. Chart 4 illustrates this by comparing, for each publication, the percentage of female authors and the percentage of space they receive.

Not all publications followed this discriminatory trend. The statistics show that nine publications - two women's and seven of the others - did not give more to those who already had more. For five of the nine the results indicate that books by men and women receive roughly the same amount of space overall. These were the *Spectator*, *Observer*, *New Statesman*, *School Librarian* and *Spare Rib*; the comparison figures in each case are within less than 1 per cent of each other. The remaining four publications - the monthly left-leaning magazine *New Socialist*, the weekly *City Limits*, the humour magazine *Punch* and the women's magazine *Options* - actually reversed the general trend by giving more space proportionally to the underdog. This means that, of those four, the first three, while preferring male authors, actually gave more space proportionally to female authors. *Options*, on the other hand, offers more space to male authors.

But percentages are abstractions and, depending on the raw data they are based on, can minimise or maximise differences. For instance, the percentages for male authors in *Spare Rib* reflect only one book review over the whole year. Thus any differences in

■ CHART 3 ■

THE SPACE BREAKDOWN

	% Space allotted Female books	Male books
Spare Rib	98.12	1.88
Company	75.51	22.68
Cosmopolitan	72.00	25.90
Good Housekeeping	65.86	31.98
Options	52.70	43.26
Woman and Home	52.30	33.92
She	50.19	39.22
City Limits	40.84	57.96
School Librarian	36.99	47.06
Fiction Magazine	32.76	66.73
Literary Review	29.05	65.92
New Statesman	28.85	65.55
New Socialist	25.11	71.45
Daily Telegraph	23.50	72.25
Punch	23.07	73.20
Observer	20.17	74.77
Listener	18.69	77.21
Times	17.25	78.70
Times Lit Supp	16.99	80.35
Sunday Times	16.93	74.80
Spectator	16.51	83.07
London Review of Books	14.79	79.75
Guardian	13.95	79.43
Marxism Today	13.91	69.01
Financial Times	13.87	80.30
New Society	13.72	76.15
Mail on Sunday	12.75	84.75
The Times Higher Education Supplement	9.58	75.52

* To highlight comparison between female and male, unknowns have been omitted

A comparison of percentages between female authors and the space they receive

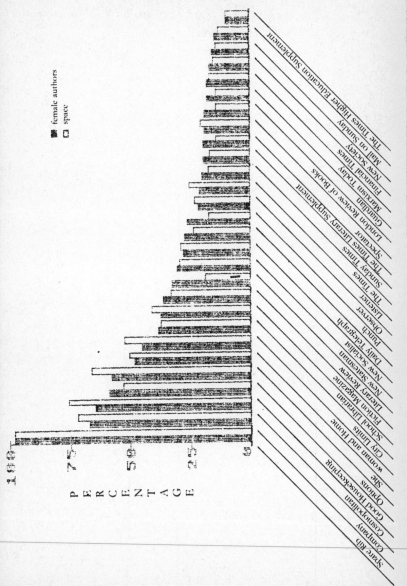

■ female authors
□ space

The Times Higher Education Supplement
Mail on Sunday
New Society
Financial Times
Marxism Today
Guardian Review of Books
London Review of Books
Spectator
The Times Literary Supplement
Sunday Times
The Times
Listener
Observer
Punch
Daily Telegraph
New Socialist
New Statesman
Literary Review
Fiction Magazine
School Librarian
City Limits
Woman and Home
She
Options
Good Housekeeping
Cosmopolitan
Company
Spare Rib

PERCENTAGE

100
75
50
25
0

The literary dinner party

15

length may be swallowed up in overall percentages. Another example of how percentages can minimise differences would be in magazines like the *Spectator*, which run such long reviews that overall figures can mask some differences. The reverse is true for publications like *Woman and Home*, which mentions books very briefly in its columns. Because of this, the differences are blown up by percentages. So, while the percentages are certainly indicative, we wanted to complement them by providing another perspective on length.

This has been done by computing the average length of a review of a man's and a woman's book for each publication. The results, in Chart 5, provide a graphic idea of the different lengths accorded men's and women's books and reinforce the trends already noted in the space percentages. While, again, some of the differences are minimal, many are striking. In the *Listener*, reviews of women's books are just under 15 square inches while reviews of men's books are almost 27 square inches. In *The Times* a woman author can expect 8.3 square inches of review compared to the 14.5 a man could expect. (Figures like these may indicate a trend towards grouping women's books together in one review.) Again, the trend crops up reversed in most of the women's magazines with the biggest gap between the sexes being seen in *Company*, where male authors receive on average about 30 per cent less review space. Such a disparity, while still marked, is not as large as those displayed by *The Times* and the *Listener*.

And, not surprisingly, those two publications are found at the top of the 'worst of the worst' list as far as discriminating against women when the figures for average length were analysed in terms of their standardised means. This calculation makes it possible to see which publications favoured women most or least. Joining *The Times* and *Listener* as publications which discriminate most against women in terms of length of review were the *Guardian*, *New Society*, *Mail on Sunday*, *Marxism Today* and *Options*. At the other end of the list - i.e. those comparitively favouring women the most - were *Company*, *New Socialist*, *Woman and Home*, *Cosmopolitan*, *City Limits*, *Good Housekeeping* and *Punch*.[3]

The outcome of the study of space shows that favouritism is rife in how male- and female-authored books are treated on the page, and that in all publications except women's magazines (with a few notable exceptions!) it is male authors who benefit. The next 'clue'

■ CHART 5 ■

WHAT'S 'AVERAGE' FOR WOMEN AND MEN?

	average length* of review		
	female authors	male authors	total authors
London Review Books	59.37	72.07	70.05
New Socialist	43.32	34.74	35.79
Literary Review	40.76	41.40	40.56
Spectator	40.00	43.44	46.95
The Times Literary Supplement	33.73	39.88	38.48
Punch	25.21	22.86	23.18
The Times Higher Education Supplement	24.16	24.91	24.05
Fiction Magazine	23.14	26.40	25.36
New Society	17.92	24.86	24.18
New Statesman	17.66	16.84	16.82
Marxism Today	16.93	25.02	23.03
Listener	14.83	26.77	23.19
Financial Times	13.71	15.88	15.36
Spare Rib	13.47	16.00†	13.51
Good Housekeeping	10.72	9.17	9.41
City Limits	9.82	8.29	8.90
Sunday Times	9.71	12.53	11.51
Company	9.38	5.75	8.01
Observer	9.09	8.80	8.78
School Librarian	8.66	8.85	8.99
Guardian	8.80	11.85	11.21
Daily Telegraph	8.55	10.85	9.91
The Times	8.31	14.47	13.51
Mail on Sunday	7.31	10.51	9.56
Cosmopolitan	5.70	4.75	5.31
Options	4.95	7.05	5.53
She	4.22	4.02	4.05
Woman and Home	3.52	2.82	3.04

* Length given in square inches
† Based on only one review

Placement percentages for male and female authors

The literary dinner party

	FIRST (%)			SECOND (%)			THIRD (%)		
	f	m	u	f	m	u	f	m	u
LITERARY									
Fiction Magazine	17	83	0	0	100	0	33	66	0
Literary Review	17	75	8	25	67	8	17	67	17
London Review of Books	0	100	0	8	83	8	0	100	0
The Times Literary Supplement	8	92	0	8	83	8	17	83	0
EDUCATION									
School Librarian	not applicable - placed alphabetically								
The Times Higher Education Supplement	0	92	8	25	67	8	17	75	8
NEWSPAPERS									
Daily Telegraph	17	83	0	17	83	0	27	73	0
Financial Times	0	100	0	25	75	0	17	83	0
Guardian	8	92	0	0	92	8	17	83	0
Mail on Sunday	8	92	0	17	83	0	17	83	0
Observer	25	75	0	8	92	0	42	58	0
Sunday Times	0	92	8	17	58	25	17	75	8
The Times	8	92	0	25	75	0	58	42	0
GENERAL									
City Limits	75	25	0	33	58	8	33	67	0
Listener	0	100	0	25	75	0	33	50	17
New Society	0	75	25	8	92	0	17	75	8
New Statesman	25	75	0	25	58	17	17	75	8
Punch	17	83	0	8	83	8	25	67	8
Spectator	8	92	0	8	92	0	8	92	0
SOCIALIST									
Marxism Today	8	83	8	8	83	8	20	30	50
New Socialist	36	64	0	27	64	9	9	91	0
WOMEN'S									
Company	83	17	0	75	25	0	42	50	8
Cosmopolitan	75	17	8	75	25	0	58	42	0
Good Housekeeping	58	42	0	75	25	0	58	33	8
Options	50	50	0	67	33	0	25	67	8
She	42	42	16	58	42	0	42	50	8
Spare Rib	100	0	0	100	0	0	100	0	0
Woman and Home	82	18	0	36	55	9	45	27	27

as to how authors are treated on the page was to find out which sex is likely to get top billing (and second and third) in a publication. To do this we examined each book section to determine the three most prominent reviews. In newspapers and magazines with only one page of reviews, the top three reviews were picked by looking at the size of headline and other factors if necessary. In publications with several pages of reviews, we counted the first three to appear. (This research did not apply to *School Librarian*, as it runs its reviews in alphabetical order.) The results, calculated as percentages, can be seen in Chart 6.

With one exception, top billing on all publications that were not 'women's magazines' went to male authors. That exception was *City Limits*, where nine of the 12 top reviews were of books by women authors. But *City Limits* joins the crowd in featuring mostly men's books in the second and third review slots.

The results in the seven women's publications were not as clear-cut. In five publications the top spot usually did go to women, but in *Options* and *She* magazines the number one review place was split between women and men authors. And, except for *Woman and Home*, the second spot was also usually reserved for women authors. But male authors were favoured for the third spot by three publications - *Company*, *Options* and *She*. In only three women's magazines - *Good Housekeeping*, *Cosmopolitan* and *Spare Rib* - did women authors persist in dominating the three top spots throughout the year. Such figures emphasise again that the sex-bias in women's magazines, while often marked, is not as strong overall as it is in the other publications.

While the results for women's magazines show that there is at least one area in which women's books are in the spotlight, the figures for the other publications tell a very different story for the woman author. For she would seem to have less chance to receive that magic invitation. And, if she should receive it, she is unlikely to get the same amount of attention in terms of length as her male colleagues. To add insult to injury, she also will probably be passed over for the places of honour. The results of this survey show a pervasive discriminatory pattern that can only serve to heighten the second-class status of women's books in most general readership publications.

2. Fact and Fiction

Male book to female book: 'So why did you get invited on to this page?'
Female book: 'I dunno. I must be the token fiction.'

The conversation above may be imaginary, but it reflects a perception that women and fiction are somehow inseparable on the book pages, the theory being that when women's books do get invited on to the review pages, they are invited only when they occupy the appropriate sphere - fiction. Whether, based on results, this theory is fact or itself fiction can be tested somewhat by looking at the trends of reviews in the 28 publications.

Before looking specifically at the place of women and fiction in each publication, however, we wanted to find out what the general trends of fiction and non-fiction were. While we don't know the percentage of fiction books versus non-fiction that end up on the literary editor's desk, the sample of books published in 1985 did at least provide a starting point in revealing that about 12 per cent were fiction.

But fiction's evident minority status is not generally reflected on the book review pages. In half of the publications - including six of the seven women's magazines, the *Listener*, *Fiction Magazine*, *School Librarian*, *Punch*, *The Times*, *Daily Telegraph*, *City Limits* and the *Mail on Sunday* - the fiction minority actually formed a majority on the review pages. The *Observer* balanced its reviews of fiction and non-fiction almost evenly with all other publications favouring non-fiction in varying degrees. (See Chart 7 for the full results.) However, the percentage of fiction books making the review pages of the 28 publications was higher than that 12 per cent in all but three cases. Assuming that the books sent out for review resemble

■ CHART 7 ■

IS FICTION THE FAVOURITE?

	percentage of books	
	fiction	non-fiction
Options	92.98	7.02
Fiction Magazine	92.31	7.69
Cosmopolitan	86.84	13.16
Company	81.58	18.42
Good Housekeeping	79.69	20.31
Spare Rib	65.08	34.92
The Times	58.13	41.88
School Librarian	56.52	43.48
Punch	54.55	45.45
Mail on Sunday	54.17	45.83
Listener	52.60	47.40
She	52.47	47.53
Daily Telegraph	51.45	58.55
City Limits	51.18	48.82
Observer	50.33	49.67
Guardian	44.16	55.84
Sunday Times	40.61	59.39
New Statesman	39.18	60.82
Financial Times	37.04	62.96
Literary Review	35.55	64.45
The Times Literary Supplement	33.69	66.31
Marxism Today	32.88	67.12
London Review of Books	29.43	70.57
Spectator	26.17	73.83
Woman and Home	22.58	77.42
New Society	9.63	90.37
New Socialist	7.55	92.45
The Times Higher Education Supplement	0	100.00

somewhat the publishing trends, the emphasis on fiction in most publications can be seen as unnatural. However, without knowing exactly how many fiction and non-fiction books are sent for review, the strength of the bias towards fiction can't be gauged.

Women do write more fiction than men. Our sample of books published in 1985 showed that women author 58 per cent of fiction books and men 38 per cent. (The remaining 4 per cent had authors of unknown sex.) But again the average book review page does not reflect this. More fiction by women is reviewed only on the pages of the seven women's magazines plus *School Librarian. New Socialist* features the same number of fiction books by men and women, but the other 19 'men's' publications stay true to their preferred author by featuring more reviews of male fiction. In some cases, this preference was marked: in the *Guardian, Financial Times* and the *London Review of Books* about three-quarters of the fiction reviewed was written by men. (See Chart 8 for the results.)

These figures highlight just how strong the preference for male authors is on most general readership publications. Given the fact that women do write more fiction - and assuming this is reflected to some degree in books sent out for review - the allegiance to men's fiction shows a stubborn adherence to their favoured-sex policy that perseveres against all numerical odds. This bias also points up the underlying message of this examination of general trends: that the realities of publishing impinge very little upon the make-up of the book review pages. If a magazine wants to review fiction, it will do just that despite the predominance of non-fiction in publishing. If a publication prefers male authors, in almost all cases it will also prefer them as fiction writers despite the predominance of women's fiction in publishing. Clearly, the strongest factor determining the make-up of the review pages is a publication's own preferences. To some extent, each produces a book review page that tells us more about the publication's biases than any trends of book publishing.

We now move from the general to the specific, leaving behind attempts to contrast reality with the books pages to concentrate instead on the intrinisic trends of each section as regards women's fiction. While we already know the larger picture - i.e. almost all men's publications prefer men's fiction while the reverse is true for women's magazines - we wanted to take a closer look at the exact role women's fiction fulfils on the review pages. Chart 9 reveals this by showing the percentages for women's and men's fiction and

■ CHART 8 ■

WHO FAVOURS FEMALE FICTION?

	percentage fiction female	male	total fiction reviews seen
Spare Rib	100.00	0	41
Woman and Home	80.95	14.29	21
Cosmopolitan	69.70	28.79	66
Company	64.52	32.26	62
Good Housekeeping	60.78	29.41	51
Options	60.38	33.96	106
She	51.76	42.35	85
New Socialist	50.00	50.00	4
School Librarian	42.67	39.74	78
Spectator	39.29	60.71	28
Fiction Magazine	38.89	61.11	36
Daily Telegraph	38.73	54.23	142
City Limits	38.46	61.54	65
Listener	38.27	60.49	8:
Sunday Times	31.09	58.82	119
New Society	30.77	69.23	13
The Times	30.11	66.67	93
Literary Review	29.67	66.45	155
Marxism Today	29.17	70.83	24
Observer	28.48	70.87	230
The Times Literary Supplement	28.31	70.78	219
New Statesman	25.37	64.18	67
Punch	25.00	69.44	36
Financial Times	20.00	76.00	50
Guardian	19.54	75.86	87
London Review of Books	19.42	76.70	103
Mail on Sunday	19.23	73.08	26
The Times Higher Education Supplement	0	0	0

Fact and fiction

	fiction			non-fiction		
LITERARY	% by females	% by males	% by unknown	% by females	% by males	% by unknown
Fiction Magazine	35.90	56.41	0	0	7.69	0
Literary Review	10.55	23.62	1.38	18.35	40.83	5.28
London Review of Books	5.71	22.57	1.14	10.86	55.43	4.29
The Times Literary Supplement	9.54	23.85	0.31	9.85	53.69	2.77
EDUCATION						
School Librarian	29.71	22.46	4.35	8.70	25.36	9.42
The Times Higher Education Supplement	0	0	0	9.54	72.92	17.54
NEWSPAPERS						
Daily Telegraph	19.93	27.90	3.62	7.25	38.04	3.26
Financial Times	7.41	28.15	1.48	8.15	49.63	5.19
Guardian	8.63	33.50	2.03	9.14	41.62	5.08
Mail on Sunday	10.42	39.58	4.17	4.17	39.58	2.08
Observer	11.82	35.67	2.84	7.66	38.95	3.06
Sunday Times	12.63	23.89	4.10	7.17	45.05	7.17
The Times	17.50	38.75	1.88	8.75	30.00	3.13
GENERAL						
City Limits	19.69	31.50	0	17.32	30.71	0.79
Listener	20.13	31.82	0.65	9.09	35.06	3.25
New Society	2.96	6.67	0	15.56	67.41	7.41
New Statesman	9.94	25.15	4.09	17.54	40.35	2.92
Punch	13.64	37.88	3.03	7.58	36.36	1.52
Spectator	10.28	15.89	0	7.48	66.36	0
SOCIALIST						
Marxism Today	9.59	23.29	0	9.59	41.10	16.44
New Socialist	3.77	3.77	0	16.98	69.81	5.66
WOMEN'S						
Company	52.63	26.32	2.63	11.84	5.26	1.32
Cosmopolitan	60.53	25.00	1.32	6.58	3.95	2.63
Good Housekeeping	48.44	23.44	7.81	9.38	9.38	1.56
Options	56.14	31.58	5.26	1.75	3.51	1.75
She	27.16	22.22	3.09	20.99	17.28	9.26
Spare Rib	65.08	0	0	33.33	1.59	0
Woman and Home	18.28	3.23	1.08	26.88	33.33	17.20

non-fiction. The results are printed for all the publications, but for analysis we were specifically interested in looking at the figures for the 13 publications that generally preferred non-fiction. (Those preferences can be seen by looking back to Chart 7.) The most popular books by men on these publications were non-fiction. Would that non-fiction trend also hold true for women's books? Or, would the 13 reverse their own preference in the case of women's books by printing more female fiction than female non-fiction? If they did reverse their own preference, we interpreted this as showing an overt bias towards women's fiction (and against women's non-fiction!).

An examination of the figures show that in all but two cases such an overt bias cannot be found. Of the 13 publications, 11 did not reverse their own preferences and indeed printed more women's non-fiction than fiction. But this consistency was broken in the cases of the *Spectator* and the *Sunday Times*. These two non-fiction-oriented publications actually reviewed more women's fiction than non-fiction, thus going against their own trends. For these three, the most reviewed books were male non-fiction followed by male fiction. Next, however, came women's fiction, with women's non-fiction in last place. This overt bias towards women's fiction and against women's non-fiction means that on these two publications, the woman author could also be seen as the token fiction author.

Although such a conclusion is only applicable outright in two cases, there are several other publications that lean towards being included. Of particular note is the *Observer*, which escaped the label only because it has no clear preference for fiction or non-fiction books and thus could not be seen as going against its own preference. *Marxism Today*, a non-fiction publication, was excluded only because it printed the same number of female fiction and non-fiction reviews. Other non-fiction publications which came near to being included were the *TLS*, the *Guardian* and the *Financial Times*. And so of the 13 non-fiction-oriented publications, only the following seven were clearly committed to women and non-fiction: *London Review of Books*, *Literary Review*, *New Society*, *New Socialist*, *New Statesman*, *The Times Higher Education Supplement* and *Woman and Home*.

(It is also of note that three of the 14 fiction-oriented publications showed a corresponding overt bias towards men and non-fiction.

They were the *Listener, School Librarian* and *Daily Telegraph*, fiction-oriented publications that nonetheless reversed their own preference by running more reviews of male non-fiction books.[1] And the *Mail on Sunday, City Limits* and *Punch* came close to displaying such a bias.)

To take a closer look at the results, the figures were reformulated in a different context. This time, men's books and women's books were treated as separate categories, each totalling 100 per cent, a computation that puts the sexes on equal footing as far as a comparison goes. For each sex of author we then totalled the percentages of fiction and non-fiction that was reviewed. By comparing the percentages for men and women for fiction, we could then take a telescopic look at which sex is more likely to be reviewed for fiction. The results, in Chart 10, showed clearly that a female author remains more likely than a man to be reviewed for fiction. This bias remains so despite all other preferences. Correspondingly, a man remains more likely to be reviewed for a non-fiction book. The only clear exceptions to this out of the 28 publications were the *New Statesman* and *Company*. On both of these magazines, a woman is more likely than a man to be reviewed for non-fiction while a man is more likely to be featured for fiction. The figures for *She* and *Literary Review* are too close to be called definitive, but on all of the other 24 publications a clear bias persists towards women and fiction.

The dimensions of this bias vary considerably among the publications. On some, such as *City Limits, Cosmopolitan* and the *Guardian*, it is a subtle preference that shows a woman is only slightly more likely than a man to be reviewed for fiction. The extent of the bias then grows larger on the rest of the publications until, at the other end of the spectrum, are found five publications in which a woman is far more likely than a man to be reviewed for fiction. Not surprisingly, both the publications found guilty of overt bias (the *Sunday Times* and the *Spectator*) are included in that quintet. Joining them are the *Daily Telegraph, School Librarian* and *Woman and Home*.[2] In the latter two cases, this can be explained somewhat by other factors: we have seen that *School Librarian* is unique among the 'men's' publications in running more reviews of fiction by women than men, and *Women and Home*'s favourite author is a woman anyway. But in the case of the *Daily Telegraph* - which favours male authors in general and male fiction authors in

TAKING A CLOSER LOOK: A COMPARISON

	female authors % writing		male authors % writing	
LITERARY	fiction	non-fiction	fiction	non-fiction
Fiction Magazine	100.00	0	88.00	12.00
Literary Review	36.51	63.49	36.65	63.35
London Review of Books	34.48	65.62	28.94	71.06
The Times Literary Supplement	49.21	50.79	30.75	69.25
EDUCATION				
School Librarian	77.36	22.64	46.97	53.03
The Times Higher Education Supplement	0	100.00	0	100.00
NEWSPAPERS				
Daily Telegraph	73.33	26.67	42.31	57.69
Financial Times	47.62	52.38	36.19	63.81
Guardian	48.57	51.43	44.59	55.41
Mail on Sunday	71.43	28.57	50.00	50.00
Observer	60.67	39.33	47.80	52.20
Sunday Times	63.79	36.21	34.65	65.35
The Times	66.67	33.33	56.36	43.64
GENERAL				
City Limits	53.19	46.81	50.63	49.37
Listener	68.89	31.11	47.57	52.43
New Society	16.00	84.00	9.00	91.00
New Statesman	36.17	63.83	38.39	61.61
Punch	64.29	35.71	51.02	48.98
Spectator	57.89	42.11	19.32	80.68
SOCIALIST				
Marxism Today	50.00	50.00	36.17	63.83
New Socialist	18.18	81.82	5.13	94.87
WOMEN'S				
Company	81.63	18.37	83.33	16.67
Cosmopolitan	90.20	9.80	86.36	13.64
Good Housekeeping	83.78	16.22	71.43	28.57
Options	96.97	3.03	90.00	10.00
She	56.41	43.59	56.25	43.75
Spare Rib	66.13	33.87	0	100.00
Woman and Home	40.48	59.52	8.82	91.18

Fact and fiction

27

particular - the marked bias is significant and, when examined in light of the other findings, it is clear that women authors on the pages of this newspaper are overwhelmingly shunted into the fiction area.

In summary, then, the survey of fiction and non-fiction has resulted in several conclusions. The first is that the reality of book publishing is not reflected in general on the books pages. More non-fiction books are published than fiction, but a publication that prefers fiction will review more fiction. The strength of a publication's own preferences are also borne out by the strong sex-linked trends. Women may write more fiction than men, but this is not reflected in an overwhelming majority of the 'men's' publications. Instead, remaining true to their favourite author, they run more reviews of men's fiction.

Yet, despite this, a bias towards women and fiction still remains. For on almost all publications a woman author remains more likely than a man to be reviewed for fiction. And when the trends are examined for the 13 non-fiction-oriented publications, we find that in two cases this bias has ballooned into an overt preference. This leaves women's non-fiction as the loser on publications where all other trends suggest it should not be. For while it should come third in popularity, it is last, overshadowed on these two publications first by men's non-fiction, then men's fiction and then also by women's fiction. But while the 'token fiction' theory is upheld only in these two cases, we have also seen that a pervasive and persistent sex-linked trend towards women and fiction does exist almost universally.

Taken as a whole, the picture is a curious mixture and it could be argued that the bias - overt or otherwise - is merely a result of women's predominance in fiction in the publishing world. If this were true, then it certainly would be an anomaly on the book review pages. For this survey has shown clearly that in general a publication reviews what it wants to, regardless of publishing trends. And such a conclusion begs the question: if this bias towards women and fiction is just after all a reflection of reality, then why isn't reality reflected in other areas as well?

For instance, take the *Sunday Times*. It prefers male authors (Chart 2) and non-fiction books (Chart 7). But when fiction is reviewed it will be written by a man almost 60 per cent of the time (Chart 8), thus revealing a stubborn adherence to its 'men first' policy even in the area of fiction. Overall, the most reviewed books are male non-fiction followed by male fiction. But this trend is reversed in the case of women authors, with the third place taken by female fiction and female non-fiction trailing last place (Chart 9). So when women do manage to get invited on to this male-oriented page, they are mostly invited for their fiction skills. This overt bias becomes clearer when a direct comparison of men's and women's books is made (Chart 10). In this comparison, with books by each sex being treated as a separate category of 100 per cent each, we see that women authors appear on the pages almost two-thirds of the time for fiction and only one-third of the time for non-fiction. Meanwhile, men appear almost two-thirds of the time for non-fiction and roughly one-third for fiction. Such results, looked at overall, show this is one male-oriented newspaper that has pigeon-holed women authors into a fiction slot. To put this trend down to a 'reflection of reality' is suspect when confronted with a newspaper which gives much more space to men's fiction despite the reality of women's predominance in this area.

This survey has shown that the *Sunday Times*, while more extreme than most in its bias, is not atypical. The male bias displayed by almost all 'men's' publications generally places women in an obscure position on their pages. And when books by women are reviewed, the preference for women's fiction leaves the female writer of non-fiction even more marginalised. The results of this survey have shown that while the 'token fiction' theory is not an across-the-board phenomenon, it is not at all just a fiction itself in the cases where marked bias is not found. Its precepts lurk on the pages of almost all publications, albeit in a more subtle form.

3. The Female Reviewer

 Authors aren't the only people who get their names on the book pages. There's also the reviewers themselves. And although the rules for getting invited to review, as opposed to being reviewed, are different, the results as far as women and numbers go are similar.

Once again it is the women's magazines that favour the females with the other 21 publications mostly coming down firmly in favour of men. The only two exceptions are *City Limits* and *New Socialist*, both of which display a balance and use about the same amount of reviewers of both sexes. (See Chart 11.) Most of the other publications remain polarised, with all the women's magazines featuring women's reviewers almost exclusively and 16 of the remaining 21 publications keeping their percentage of female reviewers at 30 per cent or lower. (The *Guardian, Sunday Times* and *The Times Higher Education Supplement* have the dubious honour of tying for last place with only 9 per cent female reviewers each.)

Female reviewers are also linked to their scribbling sisters in another, more tangible, way. For on 16 of the publications, the female reviewer mostly writes about books by women. Those publications include all the women's magazines plus nine of the 'men's' publications. (A listing of the results are included in Chart 12.) All of these nine feature more male reviewers than females, and so the minority female reviewer finds herself linked up with the minority female author. On the other 12 publications - all of them male-oriented for authors and 11 of them male-oriented towards reviewers - the female reviewer is more likely to review a book by a man. These results are especially significant because it is the only area in this survey in which a substantial number of the 'men's'

■ CHART 11 ■

REVIEWING THE REVIEWS

	reviewers			literary editor
	% female	% male	total no.	
Company	100	0	12	F
Cosmopolitan	100	0	12	F
Good Housekeeping	100	0	12	F
Options	100	0	12	F
She	100	0	12	F
Spare Rib	100	0	12	F
Woman and Home	100	0	12	F
New Socialist	51	42	39	M
City Limits	49	51	74	M
Marxism Today	44	56	43	M
School Librarian	43	57	119	-
Punch	38	62	34	M
New Statesman	30	70	91	F
The Times Literary Supplement	27	73	354	M
Observer	25	75	140	M
Fiction Magazine	25	75	16	-
Literary Review	25	75	299	F
London Review of Books	24	76	225	M
Daily Telegraph	21	79	90	M
Mail on Sunday	20	80	44	F
Financial Times	19	81	68	M
Listener	19	81	69	M
The Times	17	83	77	M
New Society	14	86	116	M
Spectator	14	86	81	M
The Times Higher Education Supplement	9	91	180	M
Sunday Times	9	91	211	F
Guardian	9	91	81	M

magazines differed with each other.

This trend could be interpreted in two ways. The linking of women authors and reviewers could be seen as creating a female ghetto on the books pages of the 9 'men's' publications that do this. On the other hand, this practice could be viewed as a progressive step that showed that the literary editors of at least these nine publications were aware that women have significantly different life experiences than men and believe that a book written by a woman is perhaps better understood and best reviewed by someone of her own sex. (Whether it is advantageous in general from an author's point of view to be reviewed by a woman remains a much discussed, but little researched, topic.)

Whatever the interpretation, the fact remains that women, whether reviewer or author, share some trends of the book review pages. On women's magazines, they are a majority and are linked together as such. On all the 'men's' publications but one, they make up a minority that nonetheless, by virtue of how reviews are assigned, are still bound together on the printed page.

❛Pay no attention to what the critics say; no statue has ever been put up to a critic.❜

Sibelius

4.   The Good, the Bad and the Ugly

The facts of life for women on the books pages contain elements of the good, the bad and the ugly. The good stems from the numbers culled from the women's magazines - which reveal a mostly fiction-oriented world where the female author is indeed the honoured guest. She is given more room and a place at the top table. The bad is that it seems that any publication that is not specifically aimed at women is tilted towards men. In most of these publications, the female author's place is minimised. She receives, on the whole, less room and a place of little distinction. In general, the publications do not give her the proper amount of credit for her talents in fiction. But she is still more likely to be invited for fiction than non-fiction. The ugly has to be that these trends are so strong in so many publications: the female author is stuck in a world of feast or famine when in fact she may just want three square meals.

This is the overall picture painted in broad strokes by the statistics of this survey. So far, the results have been analysed mainly on their own terms and a careful effort has been made to present the subtle variations in terms of numbers unique to each publication. Now, in Chart 12, those individual variations have been reduced to overall trends. While this lacks the detail of the other charts, it does provide a general picture of the trends as revealed in this research. It is organised by category, thus giving a clearer idea of how similar publications stack up against one another.

In the first category, literary publications, the favourite sex of author is male and he is favoured in terms of space and placement on all four publications. Three of the four - *Fiction Magazine, London Review of Books* and *The Times Literary Supplement* - also stay true to

■ CHART 12 ■ BRINGING IT ALL TOGETHER

	AUTHORS			FICTION/NON-FICTION				REVIEWERS	
	Sex of favourite author	Is favourite favoured in space?*	Who gets top billing?	Fiction or non-fiction oriented?	Sex of author with the most fiction reviewed	Overt bias?†	Subtle bias?‡	Sex of favourite reviewer	Who is most likely to review a female-authored book?.
Fiction Magazine	M	Y	M	Fic.	M	n/a	Y	M	F
Literary Review	M	Y	M	NF	M	N	N§	M	F
London Review of Books	M	Y	M	NF	M	N	Y	M	M
The Times Literary Supplement	M	Y	M	NF	M	N	Y	M	F
School Librarian	M	same	n/a	Fic.	F	n/a	Y	M	F
The Times Higher Education Supplement	M	Y	M	NF	M	N	n/a	M	M
Daily Telegraph	M	Y	M	Fic.	M	n/a	Y	M	F
Financial Times	M	Y	M	NF	M	N	Y	M	M
Guardian	M	Y	M	NF	M	N	Y	M	M
Mail on Sunday	M	Y	M	Fic.	M	n/a	Y	M	M

Observer	M	same	M	same	M	n/a	Y	M	M
Sunday Times	M	Y	M	NF	M	Y	Y	M	M
The Times	M	Y	M	Fic.	M	n/a	Y	M	M
City Limits	M	N	F	Fic.	M	n/a	Y	M	F
Listener	M	Y	M	Fic.	M	n/a	Y	M	F
New Society	M	Y	M	NF	M	N	Y	M	F
New Statesman	M	same	M	NF	M	N	N	M	F
Punch	M	N	M	Fic.	M	n/a	Y	M	M
Spectator	M	same	M	NF	M	Y	Y	M	F
Marxism Today	M	Y	M	NF	M	N	Y	M	M
New Socialist	M	N	M	NF	same	N	Y	F	M
Company	F	Y	F	Fic.	F	n/a	N	F	F
Cosmopolitan	F	Y	F	Fic.	F	n/a	Y	F	F
Good Housekeeping	F	Y	F	Fic.	F	n/a	Y	F	F
Options	F	N	same	Fic.	F	n/a	Y	F	F
She	F	Y	same	Fic.	F	n/a	N§	F	F
Spare Rib	F	same	F	Fic.	F	n/a	Y	F	F
Woman and Home	F	Y	F	NF	F	N	Y	F	F

* Determined by comparing percentages for favoured author and space alloted them. Figures within less than 1% are called 'same'
† A measure for non-fiction publications only, to see, as defined in Part One, whether a publication favours women's fiction over non-fiction against established trends
‡ As defined in Part One, illustrated in Chart 10. 'n/a' means that the figures indicate a trend, but not necessarily a definite one
§ Too close to call definite bias

the sex-linked trends in other ways: that is, they all run more fiction by male authors; display a bias towards women and fiction; and prefer male reviewers. The *Literary Review* stands out from the four (and indeed from most of the 28) in not showing a definitive bias towards women and fiction. The four differ from each other in only one other instance: *Fiction Magazine* and *The Times Literary Supplement* link up their minority female reviewers and authors while the other two do not.

The results for the second category, educational publications, show that *The Times Higher Education Supplement* is in line with the trends involving authors shown by most 'men's' publications. Men are favourite authors and favoured in terms of length and placement. Men are also the favourite reviewers and a female reviewer is more likely to review a book by a man. (As a non-fiction publication featuring no reviews at all of fiction, the fiction categories do not apply to the *THES*.) In contrast there is *School Librarian*, a quarterly publication for librarians that reviews books for children and teenagers, which differed significantly from other 'men's' publications. For while it favoured men as authors, it did not extend that to favouritism in terms of review length, and its policy of listing reviews alphabetically meant that placement was not an issue. It was also the only one out of the 21 'men's' publications to review more fiction by women. It did favour male reviewers and also linked its female authors and reviewers.

On the newsstands the seven newspapers featured in our survey may look very different. But, in terms of women and the books pages, they are all similar in adhering almost completely to the male-bias trends established in this survey. All favour male authors, and books by men were the favourite for the top spot. To compound their bias, all but the *Observer* also favoured male authors in terms of length. While they varied between printing more fiction or non-fiction (with the *Observer* running roughly the same amount of each), all stayed true to the favoured male author in terms of fiction. Only one paper, the *Sunday Times*, showed overt bias towards women and fiction, but three others (the *Observer*, the *Guardian* and the *Financial Times*) came close to being included in this category. And the fiction-oriented *Daily Telegraph* also stood out in terms of showing an overwhelming preference for women's fiction. All favoured male reviewers, and the *Daily Telegraph* was unique in the group in linking its female reviewers and authors.

The results for the six 'general' magazines studied show that while all prefer male authors, they then split evenly into three groups with two dogmatically favouring men, two tempering their favouritism slightly and two veering significantly away from the discriminatory trends. In the first group are the *Listener* and *New Society*, which stay true to their preferred male author in all comparable categories. *Punch* and the *Spectator* break the male mould somewhat in terms of space, although this difference is set off in the *Spectator* by its overt bias towards women and fiction. *City Limits* and the *New Statesman* also did not favour men in terms of space, but the two differed from the rest in other ways: *City Limits* featured women in its top review spot more than men while the *New Statesman* did not display any bias towards women and fiction. All six magazines do feature similar results for reviewers with all favouring male reviewers and all but one (*Punch*) tending to link female authors and reviewers.

The two socialist magazines - *Marxism Today* and the *New Socialist* - differed on several points, with the former being markedly more male-oriented on its books pages. For while *Marxism Today* displayed a male bias in all relevant categories, the results for *New Socialist* differed in three significant ways: it did not favour male authors in terms of length; it did not favour men as fiction authors; and its favourite reviewer is a woman.

In the women's magazines category, most of the sex-linked biases displayed by 'men's' publications are simply reversed in favour of female authors. There are three exceptions to this rule. *Options* did not favour women authors in terms of space and both that magazine and *She* gave up their top spot equally to men and women. Also *Company* and *She* stood out as not showing a bias towards women's fiction. (While *Spare Rib* did not favour women in terms of space, the results are based on only one review of a male book and, as such, are not necessarily indicative.) However, in other areas the women's publications all concurred: females were the favoured fiction writers and the favourite reviewer.

In summary, then, this survey has shown how 28 publications - diverse as they are - remain alike in their categorical discrimination towards a favoured sex on the books pages. Only six publications escape this indictment: *School Librarian, City Limits, New Statesman, New Socialist, She* and *Options.* These stood out in the survey as the only publications to differ from the sex-linked trends in at least two significant ways. (By this, we are referring to categories that affect all publications: space and placement preferences, the favourite fiction writer, bias and reviewers.) Of all the 28, these six can truly protest that they are not just 'men's' or 'women's' publications on their book pages. The *New Socialist* has the best record and was the only one of the six to differ in three categories. The fact that two of the six are women's magazines again highlights the relative flexibility of sex-linked trends shown by those magazines as compared to the 21 'men's' publications.

Another group of titles differed in one category. While these six - the *Observer*, *Literary Review*, *Punch*, *Spectator*, *Company* and *Spare Rib* - show a lack of rigidity in one specific area, they are still predominately sex-biased on their books pages.

Now we are left with 16 publications that adhere strictly to a sex code on their books pages. While the statistics for each do differ - and Charts 2-11 show this - they do not differ enough to change their overall categorical discrimination. Out of these 16, overall trends show that one stands out as not only following the sex-bias trends in all significant categories, but also fitting women into a 'token fiction' slot by showing an overt bias toward women and fiction and against women and non-fiction. This is the *Sunday Times*.

These, then, are the facts - the good, the bad and the ugly. We approached this survey with an awareness that while some readers of the books pages did see their content as sexist, others clearly did not. Up until now, the differing views of these two camps were, by necessity, based on opinion and perception only. Too little research had been published for it to be otherwise. So when we set out to do this survey we saw our initial task to be that of detectives - to gather evidence. In our case, that evidence took the form of the mounds of statistics that resulted from surveying more than 5,000 book reviews. And what was found among those numbers is the picture painted in Part One: a statistical portrait that is extraordinary for its clearly defined overall patterns of sex bias on most publications. This is a reflection of the artefact itself, not opinion or perception, and the charts in Part One provide a connect-the-number sketch for each publication. Some publications may not like their own particular reflection from 1985. But the only way to alter it is to make an effort to treat the sexes equally on the book review pages. Only then will the facts of life for women on those books pages improve.

Part Two

Introduction

The first part of this book reveals the facts - facts gleaned by methods already described from detailed research and presented in an easily digestible form.

But what are the processes which go to make up the final book pages of our chosen publications?

When we started this survey back in 1985 we wrote to the literary editors of a wide range of publications asking about their policy towards book reviewing. The response, predictably enough, was varied, ranging from the helpful to the downright rude.

We pressed on with the analysis and it became apparent that, in order to put our figures into context, we needed to study the various stages of a book's life on its road towards the review pages, and beyond.

To this end, in 1986 and 1987, we contacted publishers, literary editors of publications under scrutiny (so much more amenable now that they knew publication of a book was imminent), booksellers, librarians and, of course, authors. And this time we were able to ask their opinions of the whole reviewing process and its significance armed with a wealth of statistical information. The following chapters are the results of our findings.

5. *Publishers*

We began our exploration of the book review process with the publishers. Our aim was to discuss the selection of titles for review, their submission to reviewers and the likely effect of review coverage on sales. For people involved in the very public business of publishing and disseminating ideas and information, many were surprisingly reluctant to air their views in print. However, we were able to speak to a selection of 25 publishers operating in different areas of the publishing world - publishers of literary fiction and non-fiction, feminist publishers, mass-market paperback houses, publishers of specialist, STM (scientific, technical, medical) and educational books, and left-wing publishers - in order to find out more about the publishers' viewpoint.

With the exception of one publishing cooperative, each of the publishers we spoke to had a clearly identified person or department responsible for sending out books for review. In most cases the Publicity Director/Manager made the final decision after discussions with assistants or colleagues in the department. However, in a number of cases one person was solely responsible for drawing up review lists and sending out submissions. Editorial staff may be consulted when books are discussed for review, especially in the case of STM and educational publishers, where it is important that the book is sent to an academic or specialist with an in-depth knowledge of the subject-matter for review. Author's questionnaires can be an invaluable aid in finding potential reviewers for more specialised titles, particularly if the author has access to an expert in the field or has established contacts with editors of the relevant specialist journals.

So whose names are likely to appear at the top of the publishers' review lists? We started with the literary editors and asked our sample of publishers whether they automatically submit all new titles to the major literary editors. Almost half of those we spoke to do submit all new titles as a matter of course. Not surprisingly, the publishers of hardback fiction feel that the literary editors must be placed at the top of the list to receive review copies. The paperback publishers too underline the importance of the literary editors, and *The Times Literary Supplement* was singled out for special mention. The literary editors of the Sunday and daily national newspapers were identified as being primarily interested in literature with a capital 'L', although this does not discourage some publishers from submitting other categories of books to them. Feminist publishers, and those major publishers whose lists include imprints specifically for women, also submit books regularly to the major literary editors. While the literary editors do, therefore, receive review copies from a wide range of publishing houses, including books written by and for women, publishers tend to adopt the common approach of submitting mainly those titles which are deemed to be 'heavyweights' of lasting merit. In terms of women's writing this means that it is the work of female authors of established literary repute which is most likely to turn up on the desks of the major literary editors.

But what do you do if the books you publish are not considered fit meat to whet the appetites of the literary reviewers? When dealing with books of a more specialised or technical nature, publishers try to send them, as one would expect, to specialist journals. Most of the professions, such as law, medicine and architecture, have their own relevant trade journals with writers who possess the specialist knowledge required to review books in that field. Educational publishers in particular will by-pass the literary editors and the national daily papers and go straight to the educational journals, which focus exclusively on educational publishing, dealing with textbooks and with the expanding field of educational software.

Books of a more specialised nature often lend themselves to being used as the basis of a feature in a magazine or journal. Books with a particular topical or regional interest are submitted to features editors, journalists and correspondents who have a specific interest in that area. Thus beauty books are sent to beauty editors, fishing books to angling correspondents and books on regional topics to the relevant local media. The publishers do not expect necessarily to receive a full review of their publication, but a mention in a feature written around the subject of the book is very welcome.

A small but no less important group of publishers feels that its books are unlikely to be reviewed by the literary editors, nor are they likely to be featured in the mainstream press. Romantic fiction tends to be rejected out of hand by the literary editors as not being serious literature - indeed, it makes little pretence to do other than entertain the reader. Books of a left-wing political nature, even those with an impeccable academic pedigree, seem to be regarded as outside the sphere of the mainstream press and are therefore submitted to papers and journals dealing specifically with political theory and practice. A further important consideration for left-wing and women's presses is the fact that the literary editors of the national and Sunday papers are primarily interested in reviewing hardback books. Small independent publishers are thus further handicapped in the competition for space on the book review pages as they do not have the financial capacity to publish their new titles in hardback as well as in paperback.

At this point it is worth reminding ourselves that publishers are working with limited resources - their aim is to *sell* as many copies of a book as possible, and they are thus able to allocate only a limited number of free copies to be sent out for review purposes. Whereas one publisher may be inclined to be fairly liberal in despatching copies of a mass-market paperback for review, another publisher is going to be very careful when choosing recipients for an art or design book retailing at £50 and upwards. They will, however, be flexible in assessing the number of copies for review - an extra copy can usually be found if someone expresses a particularly strong interest in a title.

We then considered what happens when a publisher identifies a book as being of specific interest to women. Is this book submitted to the same reviewers as any other title on the publisher's list? All the relevant publishers in our sample had a definite policy of sending books by and for women to women's magazines for the review pages. Of the large number of women's magazines available on the newsstands, three emerge as being especially favoured by publishers' publicity departments - *Cosmopolitan*, *Spare Rib* and *Women's Review*. These three magazines in themselves illustrate the diversity and range of publications embraced by the term 'women's magazines'. Publishers distinguish between women's magazines on the basis of whether they are feminist or non-feminist. One feminist publisher, while making this distinction, sends books to both, regardless of subject-matter. A significant number of publishers, however, will identify the subject-matter of a title for review as either feminist or non-feminist, and will then send the book to the magazines in the relevant category. In this way, a book on fashion is perceived to be non-feminist, while a biography of a leading female writer and activist is regarded as suitable for submission to the feminist press. The categories need not be mutually exclusive. Features editors on women's magazines are also likely to receive copies of books dealing with their particular subject areas. Beauty, fashion and cookery spring easily to mind as the traditional subjects of features in women's magazines, but the enterprising publisher can widen the field - for example, books on general or family medicine can be sent to the 'resident' doctor. The editors of women's pages in the national daily papers and of magazine programmes directed specifically at women on the radio and television are important sources of potential review coverage - *Woman's Hour* being one of the most frequently mentioned.

It is apparent that publishers make an effort to identify as many outlets as possible for books which they feel are aimed specifically at women. Does this mean, then, that books which are perceived to be of particular interest to women are sent to the literary editors and reviewers to whom publishers normally submit their titles, and are then in addition submitted to the editors and feature writers on the women's magazines? Only two of the publishers to whom we spoke agreed that they submitted their women's titles to the literary editors of the Sunday and daily newspapers as they would any other title, and then also to the women's magazines as an extra source of review coverage. Women's magazines are perceived by the publishers to be more sympathetic to women's titles than are other sections of the media. This leads publishers to send review copies of women's titles to the editors of women's magazines and women's pages in preference to the literary editors and reviewers who would otherwise receive copies. Women's books which are written by well-known authors with established literary pedigrees will be sent to the national press for review, as we have seen, but women's titles which do not fall into the category of literary 'heavyweights' are likely to find themselves destined for the pages of the women's magazines as their only source of potential review coverage.

Having established who receives the publisher's review copies, we now turn to the question of what percentage of copies sent out for review are actually reviewed. All except one of the publishers in our sample had a clipping service which provides them with copies of reviews on a regular basis, collating all the reviews and giving an accurate picture of the number of reviews received. Yet, astonishingly, over a third of the publishers in our sample, when questioned, had no clear idea of how many of their carefully aimed review copies actually hit the target and scored a review.

When attempting to ascertain the percentage of review copies actually reviewed, we made a distinction between solicited and unsolicited review copies. The consensus of opinion was that a fairly high percentage of solicited copies do get reviews, though by no means all. A reviewer may well ask for a book and then review it because the subject happens to be topical or fashionable at the moment, but reviewing is not always left to chance; a reviewer may be prompted to review a book when the publisher follows up the book's submision with a phone call as a well-timed reminder of its existence.

Publishers, then, were optimistic, but vague, about the percentage of solicited copies which were reviewed. When pressed to give a figure they differed widely in their assessments - from as little as 15 per cent to 'nearly 100 per cent'. The lowest figure was quoted by a publisher of romantic fiction, and the highest by publishers of high quality literary fiction by established authors. Left-wing political publishers estimated their percentage of copies reviewed at a comparatively low 30 per cent, while paperbacks and non-fiction hardbacks ranged from 50 per cent to 90 per cent, the higher figures being quoted by publishers with established literary figures and well-known names in their lists.

Publishers estimated that the percentage of unsolicited review copies actually reviewed would be between 20 and 30 per cent lower than the figures for solicited copies, but there was always an element of luck involved. Financial considerations are also particularly relevant when considering unsolicited review copies - a publisher will be prepared to despatch a large number of unsolicited copies if the price is relatively low and the print run long, thus expecting fewer reviews percentage-wise than for a more expensive book where fewer but more carefully targeted copies are despatched.

As one form of publicity for a title, do good reviews on the book pages actually have a beneficial effect on sales of that title? Publishers cannot possibly know all the factors that influence the sales figures for an individual book, so we asked our sample of publishers to speculate for a moment on the likely effect of a good review on the sales figures. The overwhelming majority of the publishers surveyed felt that good reviews have a positive effect on the sales of the book. The important point is that quality and quantity must both be present. One good review is always worth having, but a run of good reviews is needed to noticeably influence the sales figures. The Sunday papers and the review pages of the national daily papers were held to be particularly important - good reviews in prominent papers with a large circulation can be expected to result in increased orders from the major bookshops. Publishers' representatives are able to use good reviews to support their enthusiasm for a title, and hence to sell more stock of that title into the bookshops after publication. An added bonus is that good reviews of a hardback book provide quotes for the jacket of the paperback and thus are valuable sales tools for the representatives, who, when subscribing paperbacks in advance of publication, rely heavily on the appeal of the jacket to book buyers. Although it is impossible to judge exactly what effect good reviews do have on sales, the publishers we spoke to felt certain that good review coverage could give a boost to the sales figures.

If good reviews are believed to have a positive effect on sales, are bad reviews deemed to have a negative effect? Two-thirds of the publishers who said that good reviews exert a positive influence on sales maintained that a bad review is unlikely to have any significant influence on sales at all. Indeed, any effect a bad review may have need not necesssarily be negative. A review brings a book to the attention of the reader, whether the tone of the review is positive or negative. If a book receives a number of reviews, some good and some bad, then it is probably the title which the reader remembers rather than the judgement of the individual reviewers. A bad review in a prominent trade journal of an STM title which implied, for example, that information contained in the book was incomplete or misleading, might adversely affect sales. However, an unfavourable review in a major paper of a hardback novel by a well-known author, while most unwelcome and irritating, would probably have a negligible effect on sales.

Can it be said that there is really no such thing as bad publicity, and that any review is in fact better than none? A resounding majority of publishers agreed that they would rather have any review coverage, even negative, than none at all. Small publishers competing for space on the review pages with the larger publishing houses stressed that any mention is better than no comment at all and underlined the fact that it can be very difficult to 'break into' the review pages of the major national newspapers. Reviews can often be non-committal in tone, and publishers notice that some reviews seem to consist of a rewriting of the blurb on the jacket together with a summary of the contents list from the book. This is more of a 'listing' than a review, since it offers no real evaluation of the book's merit, but even so it is welcome publicity. A title may be the subject of so many reviews and features that it reaches saturation level, where the readers have had their fill of the subject and no longer want to buy the book. In the end, a book may well benefit most from a mixture of good and bad reviews - after all, there is nothing like a spot of controversy to increase sales.

Do publishers feel that women's books (i.e. books by women or about issues which are of particular interest and relevance to women) are given adequate coverage by reviewers? Only two of those we spoke to felt satisfied that books are reviewed according to merit, saying that they felt that the sex of the author and the perceived market for the book were irrelevant. There was a wide divergence of opinion among the remaining publishers on this question. On the positive side, publishers were pleased with the amount of review coverage given to well-known female authors, and felt that established literary figures, whether male or female, are reviewed on equal terms and are accorded the same degree of respect by the reviewers.

Publishers are less optimistic about those women who are not established authors with the backing of major publishing houses to facilitate their arrival on the review pages, and are less certain of the welcome that will be accorded to these women. The attitude of the reviewers can be some cause for concern - they are perceived to be patronising or even hostile in some cases towards women authors, who are likely to find themselves relegated to the bottom of the literary league, appearing in composite reviews rather than being regarded as serious contenders for coverage in the more prominent reviews.

While publishers were divided in their opinions regarding the coverage given to women authors on the review pages, there was general agreement regarding the coverage given to books specifically aimed at the female reader. The consensus of opinion was that women's issues are given very good coverage in women's magazines, where a book has a good chance of being given a review or being mentioned in a feature. This opinion is supported by the fact that, as already noted, publishers submit women's titles to the women's magazines for review and are keen to use what they see as positive discrimination on the part of women's magazines in order to bring their books to the attention of the female reader.

Women's books are continually in danger of being marginalised. The publishers send STM and educational titles to specialised journals because they are perceived to be for a market which is not catered for by the general press. Similarly, publishers see that it is not easy to get review coverage in the general papers for women's titles, and so these are submitted to the women's magazines for review. The books receive better coverage here, and so fewer books are then sent to the general papers, resulting in fewer reviews of women's books appearing in the national press. Thus, in theory, the national press caters for a general readership, but in practice, 'general' seems to mean 'male'. Yet it is the review pages in the Sunday papers and the national daily press which are regarded as being the most influential in terms of sales. It is therefore important for the commercial success of women's titles that they be adequately reviewed in the general papers. The publishers who send books out for review choose the recipients carefully. They therefore have a vital role to play in helping women to claim their share of space on the book review pages.

Shân Morley Jones

6. Literary Editors

 If you consider that 52,994 books were published in Great Britain in 1985, and that a weekly publication like *The Times Literary Supplement*, which is almost entirely devoted to book reviews, only managed to review approximately 3,000 titles that year, it becomes obvious that book review pages are highly selective. And yet once the selection has been made, readers have effectively been told, of all the books published this week/month, these are the most worthy of consideration. Further, by the choice of reviewer, the length of review and the placing of the review on the page, a hierarchy of importance among the chosen is conveyed.

Our research shows that the number of books by women reviewed - across the whole range of publications covered - does not necessarily reflect the percentage of books written by women published, that books by women are treated erratically (depending on the nature of the publication and, more significantly, the literary editor's view of his or her readership), and that they are not subject to the same criteria for evaluation as books by men.

It is therefore essential to understand the processes at work behind the make-up of the book review pages, to determine at what point this anomalous treatment of books by women takes place, and why. It is only when the roots of the problem have been exposed that a way forward can be suggested.

It is the literary editor who is ultimately responsible for the appearance of the book review pages. Working alone or with a team, he or she will decide what to include where. However, behind the seemingly ordered world of the finished product, where in theory the *best* books are described and evaluated by the people best qualified to judge literary and/or academic merit, a whole host of considerations are at play. We decided, therefore, to assess the role the literary editor plays in determining a woman's place on the book pages.

How are books selected for inclusion? Literary editors on publishers' mailing lists can expect to receive review copies regularly from those particular publishers. They will also work their way through publishers' catalogues, receive unsolicited books, and act on recommendations from colleagues and regular reviewers. More nebulously, 'an editor has a whole range of informal contacts with publishers, academics, practitioners and others involved in the production of books on almost any subject. Editors can be approached informally by authors, agents or publishers to give consideration to reviews: equally, editors can learn informally of the planned or forthcoming publication of a title and may be interested in assessing such a work for review. In such situations, there is no hard-and-fast rule; only integrity, and mutual trust and respect.'[1]

At this point in the process 'purely mechanical [factors] like the non-arrival or late arrival of a book' (Philip Howard, literary editor, *The Times*) will bite. In fact, the role played by the publisher's efficiency, or lack of it, is particularly important for the women's magazines, such as *Good Housekeeping*, which work four months or more ahead of publication. As their reviewer, Susan Hill, pointed out, 'only those publishers who get *proofs* to me get reviews.'

As well as physical availability, a number of other consider-ations, apart from the perceived intrinsic merit of a book, will affect the literary editor's choice at this stage: the sheer number of titles received; reluctance, or refusal, to review paperbacks; the need for topicality; the need for novelty; the desire for entertainment value; even, possibly, the desire to keep in with certain publishers in order to benefit in return from advertising revenue. In addition, Philip Howard spoke for many literary editors when he said: 'Like most daily newspapers, *The Times* has an obsession these days with reviewing books no later than its rivals.'

As far as selecting reviewers goes, one obviously expects of a literary editor objectivity and integrity; it would be all too easy for a literary editor to seek reviews from friends, to solicit reviews from 'those whom one knows will provide a "comfortable" review . . . to ensure that a similarly sympathetic review will be reciprocated in times to come,'' and generally maintain a cosy élitism. With this in mind, J.D. Hendry continues, 'the most fundamental guiding principle of a review editor in preparing and publishing a review must be to provide a valid academic assessment of integrity and standing . . . Beyond this, one's guiding principles must be to take particular account of the range and level of readership.'

As to the process of marrying book with reviewer, this can either be a carefully planned exercise or a random assignment, depending usually on the nature of the publication. Smaller publications tend to rely on chance, using a willing reader or a member of staff who is obliged to do a certain number of reviews. In this situation there can be little control over the reviewer's suitability in terms of knowledge or background, and the reviewer may well be tempted to lean heavily on the publisher's blurb or on a cursory skim through the pages.

The literary editors we surveyed, however, spend much more time and effort selecting suitable reviewers, although here again methods vary. The women's magazines tend to have one female reviewer for all their books. In some cases, for example, at *Woman and Home*, *Good Housekeeping* and *Company*, she is solely responsible for obtaining a selection of books from publishers and selecting those she will review. *Good Housekeeping*'s reviewer, Susan Hill, said:

> 'I read, I suppose, four books to every one
> I review, and sort through and reject a
> great many more. I select what I want to
> read on the basis of 25 years' experience as
> a reviewer, personal taste and preference,
> availability of proof copies.'

Other women's magazines have a literary editor who pre-selects books and sends them to the reviewer, who then makes the final choice. At *Cosmopolitan*, for example, the literary editor, Emma Dally, said she chose a reviewer who is 'retained from between 6 months and one year. We like to have female reviewers, and preferably well-known journalists or novelists.' The books she selected for her reviewer were 'those that I think will be of interest to women', but 'I do leave it up to the reviewer to choose the final books to write about.'

At specialist journals such as *The Times Literary Supplement* or

Books and Bookmen, the literary editor plays a leading role in the selection process, but also works closely with other editorial staff. At the *TLS*, 'Publishers' catalogues from all over the world are circulated among the editorial staff and discussed at regular meetings, at which we try to identify what look like being the most important forthcoming books (or groups of books), and to choose reviewers. These discussions are supplemented by the recommendations of regular reviewers and other advisers, and also, most importantly, by a careful look at the books when they actually arrive.' Other considerations are borne in mind: *Books and Bookmen* attempted not to restrict themselves to "mainstream" books, covered by all the national papers, nor to "mainstream" publishers; but encourage, as far as possible, books from smaller, radical presses - e.g. Pluto, The Women's Press, Zed, the new Camden Press. Reviewers tended to be chosen 'very much on the basis of their scholarly/scientific reputations in the field covered by the book' (*The Times Higher Education Supplement*). Nearly all the books are specifically assigned to reviewers; some publications allow reviewers to request specific books, while others, such as *TLS*, view such requests with suspicion and seldom agree to them.

Some magazines professed even more specific policies. *City Limits* said they recieved 50 to 100 books a week and their priorities were 'first novels, small presses, imports, translations, genre fiction (e.g. crime, SF), and, more generally, books that fit with what we imagine our readers' interests to be - feminism, political theory, film criticism, visual arts, etc.' *Spare Rib* said they tried to 'cover books that are going to be fairly widely available, reasonably cheap, not too academic' and to 'include writing by lesbians, black women and Third World women'.

The specialist magazines and journals, whether literary, socialist or feminist, chose reviewers in a variety of ways; some relied on one method more than another but most used a mixture: a pool of regular reviewers, people who wrote in and offered their services, authorities on subjects who were approached and asked to review a particular book, and new reviewers (the *New Socialist*, for example, is always looking for new people, 'particularly young people and women').

The specialist magazines/publications, therefore, had a professed 'line' to follow and a specific group to aim for (determined by their perceived, and in some cases confessedly circumscribed, readership), both of which placed certain restrictions on their choices. The literary editors of the daily and Sunday papers, however, should have felt no such restrictions, since their readership is wider and more general. Indeed, they appeared to have the most scope as individuals to take a direct hand in choosing books and reviewers, and they claimed to have no criteria other than merit. The literary editor of the *Daily Telegraph*, David Holloway, stated:

> 'My method of selecting books for review
> is to choose the works that I think merit
> inclusion in the *Daily Telegraph*, in other
> words, books that interest me and, I hope,
> will interest our readers. Quite simply I try
> also to choose the most suitable reviewer.'

The literary editor of the *Sunday Times*, Claire Tomalin, tried

> 'to choose the most interesting and
> worthwhile books, or books that seem to
> form the basis for a readable and thought-
> provoking article; as to reviewers, I try to
> find people who write clearly, informa-
> tively and entertainingly and I am particu-
> larly interested in finding young and
> unknown reviewers.'

Well-known 'name' reviewers are generally allowed to select books to review, although it is not inevitable that they will be given the books they select; lesser-known reviewers are generally assigned books.

When asked about guidelines, the only ones literary editors admitted to concerned length and date required. A few journals, such as *New Socialist*, who use a high number of new reviewers, will try to eliminate unsuitable people before they write a review (either by letter or interview). The shorter the review and the less professional the reviewer, the more editing is required. The editor of *TLS* will brief reviewers, particularly for long features, and then if the feature/review is not acceptable, they will work on it together, or failing agreement, the review will be dropped. *London Review of Books* reminds reviewers that the long reviews must read like an essay, while *Marxism Today* points out that they consider themselves academic with a small 'a' and that their readers are non-specialist but motivated. The closest indication that choosing a reviewer is not quite as unbiased as it might seem came from the *Observer*, which said that by choosing the reviewer, you were, in many cases, choosing the type of review that the book would get; this was thought to be particularly true with a personality or 'star' reviewer. And as the *Spectator* said:

> 'Books once reviewed become important, interesting or amusing, occasionally because they lend themselves to a good piece without having much merit themselves.'

The location on the page is determined by various factors, depending on the publication. Most literary editors said the importance of the book was the only consideration; some balanced the importance of the book against the importance of the reviewer; others felt that if the reviewer was a 'personality' his or her importance might outweigh that of the book. Previous issues were taken into account, as were prevailing cultural interests, other publications' likelihood of reviewing the book and personal judgement.

Some publications paid no attention to balancing publishers, while others, possibly with an eye to advertising, made an effort to maintain a balance, or to include publishers who had been helpful. Many knew which publishers were most likely to provide titles which would interest them, and which were least likely to do so.

Thus, the picture presented by the literary editors themselves is the wholly commendable one of a group of serious-minded people choosing books and reviewers solely on merit, taking many factors into account before coming to their decision, and who, as a result, should be producing a book page or review journal which is a balanced and representative sample of a wide range of writers in different fields from a wide range of publishers.

And yet, as the results of our survey show, something has gone awry: frequently the stated philosophy of the literary editor does not tally with the reality of his or her pages. We decided, therefore, to investigate the reasons behind this discrepancy.

The group which promotes women most consistently is

women's magazines. Most of them have a very clear idea of their typical reader and deliberately try to choose books which those readers will like; they prefer not to write unfavourable reviews, try to maintain a balance of interest, and tend towards fiction rather than non-fiction. Female authors predominate, and although not all editors want to be seen espousing an anti-male preference, they are conscious of the reasons for the make-up of their pages: they know their market and they respond accordingly. 'Probably slightly more books by women are reviewed *at a guess*, merely because I get more by women' (*Good Housekeeping*); in fact, the proportion was two women authors to one man. *Spare Rib* states quite clearly that 'its reviews are nearly 100 per cent by women, and 100 per cent of our reviewers are women.' The women's magazines, then, whether traditional or feminist, are aimed clearly at a definite target group, and their reviewing practice and their book pages reflect this.

However, once we leave the world of women's magazines, we enter a more confused area, where the prejudices and difficulties facing women begin to surface. At the time of our survey there were two literary magazines staffed entirely by women, *Books and Bookmen* (despite their name!) and *Literary Review*. It was no surprise that their philosophy reflected this fact. Although we did not survey *Books and Bookmen*, it is worth mentioning their policy towards male/female writers and reviewers:

> 'As an all-woman team. . . we appreciate
> how easy it is for male reviewers, male
> authors to dominate in the magazine, and
> make particular efforts to try and achieve a
> balance between men and women.
>
> In addition, we are concerned not to
> marginalise particular reviewers or parti-
> cular interests, by confining certain
> reviews to certain areas: e.g. it is not our
> policy that women's writing should be
> reviewed only by women, or black writing
> by only black reviewers.'

In terms of the percentage of specialist books written by women which are published, *Literary Review* is one of three literary magazines that review at least the equivalent number of books by women (the others are *School Librarian* with 38 per cent and *Fiction Magazine* with 35 per cent). *Literary Review* also deliberately give male reviewers books by women to review and vice versa.

The Times Literary Supplement and the *London Review of Books* review a very low percentage of books by women (19 per cent and 17 per cent respectively) and are both aware of the imbalance between female and male reviewers (24 per cent and 10 per cent respectively). The editor of the *TLS*, Jeremy Treglown, agrees that certain pages are very male-dominated and he encourages his staff to rectify this when possible; he also tries to avoid giving women reviewers women's issues, although he is aware that someone looking at the book pages would suspect this was not the case. The same holds true for *LRB*. Both publications say that they consciously search for more female reviewers, but find it difficult to discover enough women who are specialists. *The Times Higher Education Supplement*, as might have been expected, reflects even more clearly the imbalance in the numbers of women in higher education. Only 9 per cent of books reviewed are by women; 9 per cent of the reviewers are women. The editor, Brian Morton, expressed his desire to improve on this performance, especially as 11 per cent is the figure generally quoted for the proportion of female academics, but whichever figure you use, and however lamentable it is, the ratio is a reflection of the actual situation.

The two socialist publications had very definite, and often divergent, views. Both aimed to provide a balance of male and female reviewers and do in fact come close to achieving their aims (*New Socialist*, 51 per cent women; *Marxism Today*, 44 per cent women.) The reviews editor of the *New Socialist*, Stephen Pope, has very definite ideas about allocating books to reviewers. He feels that the male sphere includes global policy, unions and labour policy; women are apt to be given art, culture, sexual politics and feminism. He deliberately tries not to let men review feminism; in the few cases where men are chosen, they are often gay. He feels that this traditional division is partly to do with age: older men like heavy politics, younger women go for feminism. Reviewers' requests to review specific titles tend to confirm this theory. *Marxism Today*, on the other hand, tries to avoid asking women to cover only women's issues. However, they are aware that this is a clear break with expected norms and is, therefore, difficult to do. In terms of books written by women reviewed in these two publications, they both achieve less favourable results (*New Socialist*, 21 per cent, *Marxism Today*, 19 per cent). *Marxism Today*'s Sally Davison gives reasons for this: 'in spite of much discussion it is still quite a male-orientated magazine. This is for two main reasons. Firstly, it deals in the world of politics with a capital "P" and is quite heavy. Secondly, in the interests of "professionalism" we tend to go for well-known authors, particularly journalists and academics, and there are far more men than women in this area.' In addition, feminism and feminist issues are considered 'light-weight' politics and not thought to be in the same league as traditional male politics: 'a biography of a suffragette, for instance, would not be considered comparable to that of a male political figure'

The general interest magazines vary considerably in their attitudes. *City Limits* has a high proportion of female reviewers (49 per cent) and a good coverage of women writers (37 per cent): 'Overall, we use roughly equal numbers of male and female reviewers: in fiction, women probably review more than men; the other way round, unfortunately, for non-fiction.' Harriet Gilbert, literary editor of the *New Statesman*, (27 per cent female writers, 30 per cent female reviewers) worries constantly about the lack of female reviewers and tries on principle to include them whenever possible. However, their subject matter - 'heavy' politics, war and foreign policy - is definitely male-dominated. If a book is of particular interest to women it will be given to a female reviewer; she sees no point in giving, say, a book of lesbian poetry to a man. With mainline fiction, no such distinction is made.

The further down the scale in terms of balance the journal was, the less aware of a problem the literary editor seemed to be. Mark Amory of the *Spectator* (17 per cent female writers, 28 per cent female reviewers) declared: 'Discrimination positive or negative plays no part.' Tony Gould of *New Society* (18 per cent female writers, 18 per cent female reviewers) said: 'The sex of the reviewer is not an issue (except perhaps in my recent Feminist Books issue, where all the reviewers were, in fact, women).'

On the whole, though, apart from women's magazines, most of the journals acknowledged there was a problem in the numbers of women they featured, both as writers and reviewers. To summarise, their explanations were varied: they talked of the low numbers of women in academia, and in the professions generally; they stressed that reviewing is very much a spare-time job, and that spare time was something that women did not seem to have much of; they pointed out that in the real world, 'heavy' and serious matters were not for women; and several came up with the argument about not wanting to marginalise women's issues. They had to be guided by the needs of their readership, and, boiled down, they blamed the system, which left women behind.

What is most interesting, however, is the attitude of the newspapers, where readership surely must be more balanced between the sexes, for it is here that the divergence between stated philosophy and reality is most apparent, yet it was here that we tended to receive blank denial of any imbalance at all. It was not particularly surprising, for instance, that the *Financial Times*, which might be expected to have the most specialised readership of all the papers, did in fact come near the bottom of the table of women authors (15 per cent). But for all their specialised readership, they still featured more female reviewers than the *Sunday Times* or the *Guardian* and more books written by women than the *Mail on Sunday*. David Holloway, the literary editor of the *Daily Telegraph*, who stated quite blithely, 'At a guess I should have thought I use as many men as women reviewers . . . but I am certainly not going to bother to count', comes out with a score of 21 per cent. The *Sunday Times* feels that their proportion of women writers reflects the number of review copies the paper receives, although in fact, at 20 per cent, their score is below the general figure of women-authored books published. Despite having a non-specialist readership and sele..ion of books, they blame the low proportion of female reviewers on the lower number of female academics, especially at Oxbridge. The *Guardian*, surprisingly, reflects probably the greatest discrepancy between philosophy and reality. Their fiction is reviewed by a regular panel which includes one woman and three men who review on a rotational basis. They firmly believe that there is no discrimination and, what is more, if there were they would hear about it. In fact, only 18 per cent of the books they review are by women and they foot the table of reviewers with only 9 per cent women. As to letters of complaint, the following deserves quotation in full:

> 'Sir, - I am at a loss to understand why, in
> this week's Books Page, there should be a

section subtitled "women writers". It implies that women are a sub-group of writers despite the fact that they contribute in equal numbers, compared with men, to our literary culture.

The odd thing is that there are two other women reviewed on the page, Marilyn French and Emma Tennant. Why were they left out of the women's section? Aren't they really women? Or is it the case that when women writers become successful they become discernable from other "women" writers and so qualify for honorary membership of the male literary élite?"

The *Mail on Sunday* felt there was no bias one way or the other (20 per cent female reviewers, 15 per cent female writers), but would not be interested in striking a balance; they felt they were writing, not for men, not for women, but for an asexual being. And here we have the key to the problem.

Women's magazines define their readership, obviously, as women, and construct their pages accordingly. The vast majority of specialist journals saw that there was a problem, but felt that they could only work to overcome it within the confines of the demands made upon them by their readership, and that readership was specialised enough to reflect current imbalances against women in the world of the professions, academia, politics, etc. But the newspapers, the group which should surely be aiming to reach people across the whole range of society, the group most avidly supplied with review copies by all the publishers, are the very ones who see no problem and are mildly amused by enquiries such as ours. In practice, they consistently review disproportionately low numbers of books by women, using disproportionately low numbers of female reviewers. What has happened is that, when talking of her 'asexual' reader, the *Mail on Sunday*'s literary editor has stumbled on to an idea expressed succinctly by Dale Spender:

'Men are in charge of our society ... their positions and resources enable them to be

the "experts" who make the pronounce-
ments on what makes sense in society, on
what is to be valued ... It should not
therefore be surprising that these influential men should consider their own frame
of reference - based on their own experience and values, which include seeing
themselves as centrally important to
society - as the basis for their judgements."[4]

The 'asexual' reader is a man. Seen in this light, everything else
falls into place.

Lesley Levine
Sally MacEachern

**❝Fortunately the 'best
sellers' are the
worst survivors.❞**

Athenaeum

7. Booksellers

For many of us there are few greater pleasures in life than spending an afternoon browsing in a bookshop - not necessarily with the intention of buying anything. The urge to buy often becomes uncontrollable, though, especially when we come across that new novel which was so well reviewed in last Sunday's paper. Of course, we may buy a book we have never heard of before, but our purchase might still owe a lot to a book review, albeit indirectly.

According to a Book Marketing Council survey, 'impulse buying' accounts for some 55 per cent of total bookshop sales. Obviously, those impulses can only be created in response to books which are actually on display. Thus, the buyers who select the shop's stock set limits on what we may buy 'on impulse'. By providing the books we see in their shops, book buyers have a great influence over our reading habits, but what influences them? Do they read book reviews, and if so, do those reviews have any effect on their choice of stock?

We spoke to a number of booksellers with responsibility for buying stock for their shops, working in very different types of bookshops ranging from small locals to the large, general bookshop. We explored the ways in which they were influenced by book reviews in their work and whether their customers were motivated to buy particular titles because of review coverage.

All the buyers made the point that review coverage could not influence decision-making about their initial subscription to a new title as most buying is done at least two months in advance, well before any reviews of a book have appeared. However, if a book has previously been published elsewhere - in the United States, for example - then the resultant review coverage may well be used by the publisher's representative as a selling point. Review coverage which has been promised in advance is often used as another tool of persuasion.

Most publishers' representatives do use the size of the publicity and promotion budget as a selling point, and if a large amount of money is being spent on promoting a title, many buyers are likely to order in larger quantities than they may otherwise have done. If no expense is spared in promoting a title, then more review copies will be sent out, thus creating greater potential for actual review coverage.

One of the buyers pointed out that 'alternative' publishing ventures - i.e. feminist, left-wing, black, etc. - tend to be smaller and often under-capitalised, and therefore have less money to spend on promotional activity, which correspondingly reduces the likelihood of their having regular access to review coverage.

Reviewers can certainly have an effect on what a buyer will order when a book appears in a paperback edition. Quotations from the reviews of the original hardback are often included as part of the blurb on the new jacket. A favourable comment from a reliable source can certainly influence a buyer to order greater quantities of the paperback version, although buyers are much more likely to be influenced by an attractive jacket design and the general appearance of the book than by any text on the jacket. It is the jacket design which first attracts the attention of a customer browsing through a display of books. Having picked the book up, the customer then turns it over to read the blurb on the back which has an important influence on the decision to buy the book or return it to the display.

All the buyers we spoke to were conscientious in their study of book reviews and regularly read the review pages in at least one Sunday paper. Many bookshops subscribe to the quality Sunday newspapers for on-the-job reading. Other sources regarded as useful, if not essential, tools for the bookseller included the *Literary Review* and the weekly book pages in the *Guardian*, *The Times* and the *Daily Telegraph*.

Those buyers working in specialist bookshops paid great attention to the reviews in the relevant specialist journals, and were clearly influenced by them. One buyer who works in a left-wing bookshop said that she regularly monitored all the major left-wing journals - *Marxism Today*, *New Statesman* and *New Socialist*, for example - and claimed that if a book which was not already in stock was reviewed in any of these publications, then it would almost certainly be ordered immediately.

Another bookseller maintained that book reviews had a direct effect on sales:

> 'Sometimes, I might be worried that I've been over-enthusiastic in buying large quantities of a particular title, but as soon as I see the book is getting reviewed - I breathe a sigh of relief and feel confident that it will sell.'

In small, local bookshops resources are limited and buying requires very fine judgement, particularly in the case of new hardback titles. One buyer commented that she was therefore very aware of the effect of book reviews, not least because her customers often mention having seen a review of a book that she has previously decided not to stock. She was very likely to order a new title as a direct result either of seeing a review herself or of a customer bringing the review to her attention.

The same buyer also referred to what she termed the 'subliminal effect' of book reviews. Often, a customer may have been interested by a review of a book, but may not actually intend to buy it. However, if the customer then sees the same title on display in a bookshop, the combined effect of having read the review and the urge to buy on impulse may become irresistible.

All the book buyers to whom we spoke agreed that book reviews do have an effect on sales. In some shops, customers regularly arrive clutching copies of papers or magazines, wanting to buy copies of a book they have seen reviewed.

In London, the book reviews in *City Limits* appear to have a significant influence on sales, and customers often ask for books which have appeared in their 'bestseller' list. Several of our book buyers said that they regarded the books pages of *City Limits* as a useful way of finding out about some of the latest titles from the less mainstream publishers. Many of the smaller publishers cannot afford effective representation and rely on such coverage of their titles as a means of increasing booksellers' and customers' awareness of their existence. There was a complaint, however, from one of the buyers about what she felt was a tendency towards political bias in *City Limits*'s book reviews:

'I sometimes feel that little attempt is made
to judge a book objectively according to
its literary merits, but that the reviewer is
more concerned with pointing out
whether the author's political stance is
compatible with their own.'

One observation made by our book buyers was that reading book reviews was essential to them if they were to successfully interpret customers' often vague enquiries. It appears that many customers *do* read book reviews, but then forget much of the detail, including the title and the author. Armed only with scant detail - 'I know it had something to do with South America' - the bookseller embarks on a complicated guessing game until the required title is hit upon. It obviously helps if the bookseller is familiar with the reviews in question.

Customers are equally, if not more likely, to be influenced by what they have heard on the radio or seen on television. A mere mention of a book's title on a popular radio programme can lead to a multitude of enquiries. Bad timing can have a devastating effect on sales, complained one buyer. If a book is reviewed ahead of publication, this can create a large demand for the book before it is available. By the time the book actually appears in the shops, the interest caused by the review will have disappeared.

When asked whether women's books - i.e. those by women or about issues relating to women - were given adequate coverage by reviewers, the response from buyers was varied. One buyer felt that those women authors who were already well-established tended to receive positive review coverage, but that less well-known women authors tended to be ignored, certainly by the mainstream press, and it was often only the 'feminist' magazines who gave them the coverage they warranted.

Some felt that books in general were not given adequate coverage, while one buyer felt that women's books in particular were not adequately reviewed. Other booksellers disagreed with this point of view and felt that the coverage given to women's books was adequate. One male buyer linked the amount of review coverage accorded to women's books with the number of women's books being published, and saw the lack of review coverage as a reflection of the small numbers of such books published rather than as an indication of bias on the part of the media.

From the results of our discussions with book buyers, it emerges that book reviews do have a substantial effect on what books people choose to buy. This works both directly and indirectly. The consensus was that both good and bad reviews had a positive effect on sales, as any coverage raises the level of awareness of a book's existence. When review coverage is good it can have an outstanding effect on the sales of a book, especially in the case of those small publishers who do not have the sales and marketing capacity of their larger competitors.

If reviews do have a substantial influence over which books people buy, then until female authors are given adequate review coverage on the book pages, they will be unable to attain their rightful share of the market.

Katharine Harding

8. *Librarians*

Once upon a time, not so long ago, libraries all across the land were buying books, lots of books. In those days, about 30,000 titles a year were being published in Britain. Now, times have changed - more than 50,000 titles a year are published in Britain alone and libraries have less, much less, money to spend. They are expected to provide more services and are able to provide fewer new books.[1]

It would seem that here, in the careful decisions which put books on to library shelves, the book review would come into its own. After all, librarians come to hear of the many new publications through promotional material, or see them listed weekly in the *Bookseller* and *British National Bibliography*; they have an overview of the year's output of titles in the annual cumulations of these services; if they miss them first time round, they can find over 250,000 titles listed in *Books in Print*. From the veritable feast of publications available, they must choose which books will best serve their wide-ranging and varied readerships, which will tempt fickle appetites and which will provide solid sustenance.

Let us look at how they are chosen by librarians to fill the shelves, and how readers then select from what is available - and where book reviews fit into these processes.

The selection process will vary in its details among borough, county and district authorities throughout the country. As they are financed by local government rates, to which all members of the community contribute, public libraries should provide books (and other services) for all tastes and for all groups within the community. The librarian aims to have a balanced, quality, current collection, one which will provide maximum choice and at the same time get maximum use. What librarians must bear in mind when choosing new titles are the existing collection, the expected readership and the money available.

In public libraries book selection is usually done by a team of subject specialists, reference librarians and branch librarians. They meet regularly to consider which books are to be purchased, and in these meetings 'someone might say they've seen that book well reviewed, or not well reviewed, and we might decide to get it, or not - but that's usually for borderline choices.' Orders are coordinated centrally, usually by a stock editor, who ensures titles are neither over- nor under-represented among branch libraries.

The 'approvals' system is much used for book selection in public libraries. Manchester, for example, does 75 to 80 per cent of its selection this way; the London Borough of Camden estimates 50 per cent of buying is from approvals. This has become an increasingly important method of book selection in the last few years. Copies of books from a range of publishers are regularly supplied by bookshops or library suppliers either on specific request or according to a brief or on the bookseller's own initiative.

The number of titles 'depends on how much there is, it's different at different times of the year, a flood of autumn books, for example, and then sometimes it becomes a trickle', reports a supplier. One library estimated an average of 200 a week. How many of these they bought depended on budget, type and suitability of material:

> 'It's easier to buy fiction on approval - we
> tend to see more of it. The publishers are
> more obliging in letting us see it; they're
> not so keen on sending technical books
> round.'

Another Inner London librarian said they get 'mostly popular stuff and light fiction' on approval. Others have commented that it's especially important to get children's books on approval: 'this can be a very sensitive area and we like to look at the book carefully before we buy it.'

'I prefer to see the material rather than read someone else's opinion of it, or have to choose just on the basis of a title and an author's reputation.' Another advantage of library suppliers is that they will process the books - adding shelfmarks, jackets, tickets, date due slips - saving considerable work and library staff time; or they give discounts. Cost-conscious libraries consider this carefully when choosing their suppliers.

Though the approvals system is convenient and works well for general books, some libraries increasingly rely upon their suppliers to do the book selection for them. The large suppliers aim to provide 'a kind of one stop shopping for British books.' The smaller suppliers, while representing different ranges of publishers, often pre-select from publishers' lists - hence some librarians feel the approvals system narrows the range of books available. By relying on suppliers, there is a danger of libraries missing out on the publications of small publishers and professional and government institutions - material which does not offer the library supplier an adequate profit margin. There is thus a need also to use other sources of supply for library materials.

These sources are often bookshops, either locals or specialists. They are chosen for their good shelf stock in certain subjects, for their quick service, foreign purchasing links, the technical knowledge and reliability of the staff. Community bookshops are frequently used as information points - their expertise at building a coherent stock is used by librarians (and others) - but orders may be placed elsewhere. One London borough uses a selection of local booksellers rather than library suppliers - each is responsible for showing certain publishers' ranges of titles. There are emergency situations: the opening of a new branch library in Yorkshire involved 'a binge in the local bookshops, buying off the shelves - but we don't do that too often.'

Along with their traditional subject collections built up over the years - history, business, etc. - which support research and attract specialists, public libraries have developed new specialisations out of the outward-looking, community-relations-orientated approach. In these, books are selected for their impact on particular groups of readers. Librarians who are selecting books in the areas of minority interests such as ethnic collections to suit the local community, young adult fiction, women's press and other 'feminist' books, gay and lesbian books need to use sources in addition to the traditional ones. Browsing expeditions in specialist bookshops and booklists from other libraries and specialist suppliers, e.g. Airlift for American feminist fiction, are felt to be the most useful methods.

When they are unable to see the actual book, some libraries find publishers' catalogues and publicity useful for alerting them of new titles, though in others 'they go straight into the bin - we just don't have time to look at them, we get most of what we need from our suppliers.' Public libraries find ordering from publishers a time-consuming process and usually go through a bookshop. Catalogues are used as a last resort, mainly for specialist, obscure or foreign material not readily available through suppliers or bookshops.

Two 'selection tools' commonly found behind the scenes in libraries are *British National Bibliography* and the *Bookseller*. *BNB* is much used in libraries for alerting of new titles and later to make sure titles have not slipped through the selection net. A recent market survey showed that 77 per cent of UK libraries use *BNB* for book selection.'

The *Bookseller* is widely used, not only to keep up with new developments in publishing. Its checklist of 'titles of the week', a round-up of publishing activity, is scanned conscientiously in many libraries, lest any possible titles be missed. Along the way, the features and - especially - advertisements in the *Bookseller* may provide a subliminal channel for popular materials to 'choose themselves'.

In addition to such 'alerting services', three review journals are particularly aimed at librarians. *The Times Literary Supplement* is designed specifically for librarians, though more used in academic libraries than in public libraries. It covers about 50 books a week, mainly from the humanities and social science fields. It suffers from timelag problems. *British Book News* is aimed at stimulating British book sales overseas, and in Britain is more respected than read. Before its recent reformatting it had reviews by specialists of about 220 titles a month in all subjects.

> 'We use that more for keeping aware, rather than for the practical nitty-gritty of choosing and ordering - your time gets too concentrated to be able to pay attention to all the reviews.'

The *Good Book Guide*, produced by a bookseller, is an alerting service for general books. Its brief reviews cover a wide scope in the 'recreational' area, which accounts for most public library lending.

Librarianship journals are not much used in British public

libraries, in contrast to the United States, where publishers have noted a direct relationship between a good review in *Library Journal* or *Choice* and sales by library suppliers.[3] Library journals with equivalent wide coverage and reputation for reviewing 'the best of the best' do not exist in Britain.

Given publishers' tendencies to increased numbers of titles and reduced print runs, new titles must be selected fairly soon after publication to be sure that they are not reported out-of-print. Timely reviews aid this process, given that reviews are most useful for selecting titles about which there is some doubt, due perhaps to the book being expensive or very specialised. Unfortunately, the reviews most useful here, those in the professional or specialist journals used by librarians responsible for particular subjects, suffer from timelag, as editors match the 'right' reviewer to the book and wait for the return of the review. Six months' to a year's delay is not uncommon. Initial reliance on reviews as a selection tool is thus not advisable, but reviews can be used as a check on book selection to ensure that all important titles have been considered.

Newspaper reviews function as pointers to likely public demand, and are suggested to be 'a useful secondary tool' for library selection - their coverage is not full enough for public librarians to use them as a regular source of selection information.

Even though review coverage is small when measured against the total number of publications relevant to a public library,

> 'the problem is often one of too much selection material rather than too little. Selection materials from many different sources present problems for the librarian. Often several announcements of the same book appear and time is wasted on selection as the result.'

Seeing a book mentioned again and again seems to mean more than what has been said about it. Number of reviews has been shown to be a better predictor of library purchase, more than favourableness of reviews.[6]

What do librarians themselves say about their use of reviews?[7] Reviews only seem to come into selection via the back door, through librarians' personal reading, out of work time:

> 'we don't use reviews in any systematic
> way; we have circulation lists for periodi-
> cals that carry reviews, but I find they get
> to me too late anyway'

> 'we don't select from reviews but perso-
> nally we do read reviews'

> 'there may be those who make sure to
> order things they've seen reviews of in
> their own reading, in the Sunday papers'

Keeping up with book reviews is one of those out-of-work-hours
activities that many librarians regard as part of their professionalism.

A textbook for student librarians states that

> 'achievement of a comphrehensive cov-
> erage of new titles is left more to luck than
> to judgement. . . selection is often made
> without full consideration of all available
> sources. In particular, little attempt is
> made to evaluate new novels; fiction
> reviews are rarely consulted. Speed and
> ease of supply is deemed more important
> than finding out what is worth buying.
> Known authors are favoured to the disad-
> vantage of new talents.'[8]

Encouragingly, for non-fiction 'there is usually machinery to
ensure that all new titles are represented and the selection of
individual titles is given more attention.' The view from the
working world is slightly different:

> 'reviews don't add that much to the human
> network that's already in operation.
> Informal networks are there in library
> systems, it's the nature of the people who
> work in them.'

Which sources of reviews do librarians actually use? Respondents to a questionnaire circulated with the Women in Libraries newsletter cited *Spare Rib*, *City Limits* and the *Guardian* as good sources of reviews. One person felt that these gave 'fair coverage to women's writing'. Other sources of reviews given were: *Sunday Times*, *TLS*, *Women's Review*, *Observer*, *New Society*, *New Statesman*, *Books and Bookmen*, *British Book News*, *American Book Publishing Record*, *Time Out*, *New Internationalist*, *China Now*, *Multicultural Teaching*. The stock editors contacted confirmed that a variety of sources was used centrally and throughout the system: *BNB* (some 'quite a bit' and some 'mostly as a backup'), the Sunday papers, the *Bookseller*, *British Book News* 'occasionally', *Aslib Book List*, though 'that gets filed quickly', *Publishers' Weekly* ('livelier than the *Bookseller*'), *Radical Bookseller*, *The Times Education Supplement*, *Australian Book News*.

It has been shown that 20 per cent of a library's stock generates 80 per cent of its loans.[9] This is the material that seems to select itself - the unmissable, well-publicised non-fiction title, and the latest well-known author. Who would dare to by-pass the latest Catherine Cookson or Dick Francis? Information given by the title, reputation of the publisher and of the author (as mentioned above), augmented by a knowledge of the library's stock and the library's users - these are the factors that count for most in book selection - not the evaluative component of critical review. As one librarian said:

> 'We don't go so much on evaluative reviews, just if the book looks like it's going to be useful; we like publishers' blurbs best, they have all the information on them, the bibliographic details we need to know for ordering. When we choose books we go by experience - we know what gets taken out.'

Yet there is research - though a pilot study done in 1978 is all that is available - which gives figures on the extent reviews are used in libraries generally.[10] Sources of suggestions for book purchases were 35 per cent from publishers' and booksellers' lists: 11 per cent from book reviews (52 per cent from staff and 48 per cent from users); 10 per cent from approvals; 19 per cent 'not known', which the study says were 'mainly the suggestions from library users'; and 15 per cent 'other'. Of those 11 per cent of suggestions arising from book reviews, 82 per cent were ordered, 9 per cent were already in stock, 2 per cent were not ordered, and 7 per cent were ordered on approval. That would mean one in ten titles ordered has been prompted, or influenced, by a book review.

We need not be too hasty in assigning book reviews to a negligible role in library book selection. The financial climate is worsening - some libraries had not been able to buy anything 'for months' before the end of the financial year. Staff - mostly overworked and underpaid non-professional staff - must be paid; wages bit into the materials budget.[11] Less money is available, the average price per book rises, and fewer books are bought. Especially for expensive titles and multiple copies, careful decisions are made, stock rationed and coordinated between branches. In this process, reviews, whether specifically searched out or merely remembered, are needed and used.

Now that we've seen how they choose books, let's turn to the practicalities of libraries in operation and see how reviews affect the readers. Who, besides you and me, are these readers? One survey found them to be 62 per cent female, 38 per cent male, with 35 per cent over 60 years of age.[12] We cannot generalise from one part of the country - or city - to another, though; libraries which do community profiling recognise this and seek to determine what groups constitute their users. For years now they have aimed to 'cater for the greatest possible number of minorities'.[13] This has proved more practicable under some governments, especially local governments, than under others. It has been estimated that, overall, one-third of the general population borrows from the public library.[14]

When you visit the library, do you dally among the reference shelves, or hurry to the 'returned books' hoping by chance to find a recent bestseller, or go directly to a specific section, be it thrillers or poetry, travel or the cinema or the stock market? Or are you likely to take pot luck among the general fiction? Perhaps your books are among the 46 per cent chosen by browsing, and like most readers you rely largely on the publishers' blurbs to make your choice.[15] Perhaps you have favourite authors in mind and look for those.

A recent survey of fiction-readers in Kent confirmed that

browsing is the most popular method of finding books, though it 'may be forced on the reader who has been unable to find the books s/he was looking for originally'. Only four of the 135 respondents specifically mentioned reviews as a factor bringing an author to mind while browsing - 'very few people go into the library to look deliberately for authors new to them'.[16] Getting new fiction on to the shelves quickly is important - though relatively few people use the reservation system for fiction, queues for the much-touted titles soon build up.[17] One library authority's selection policy states:

> 'excellent though [the work of the handful
> of very popular authors] may be it is
> probably no better than that of many
> others who do not receive the same degree
> of publicity and promotion;'

they are 'not obliged to buy the very large number of copies that would be necessary to satisfy all requests.'[18]

When it comes to selection of fiction by author only,

> 'both librarians and booksellers do it . . .
> possibly borrowers influence this in that if
> they like an author they tend to read all his
> [sic] books whether they are good or
> bad.'[19]

Though in fiction buying 'known authors are favoured to the disadvantage of new talents', 90 per cent of sales of first novels are to libraries.[20] In 1982 Tameside libraries were buying

> 'a minimum of five copies of novels of
> serious intent. . . .This is especially
> important in the case of first novels, whose
> authors nowadays depend almost wholly
> upon public library purchases for encou-
> ragement in their writing careers.'[21]

Are these new authors likely to be read? They will be part of the 'serious novels constituting 20 per cent of the fiction issued for borrowing'.[22] A survey carried out in 1978 suggests that most 'serious' fiction *is* reviewed - '82 per cent of serious fiction received at least one review in the main reviewing papers - established authors (89 per cent) being better reviewed.' Those who select their fiction by genre will be interested to read that 'mysteries' also received good review coverage. On the other hand, review coverage of 'westerns' and 'romances' was virtually non-existent, while coverage of 'historical romances' and 'family sagas' was sketchy. [23] It may not make much difference - the Kent survey found that 46 per cent of fiction books were taken out because of the author's name - many people want to read more of the same. They discover new authors by browsing - and reading the blurb - not by reading reviews. It was knowing something about the author - not about the book - that increased the likelihood of the reader being satisfied with the book. [24]

How did those frustrated borrowers know what to look for? One in two fiction readers sometimes follows up personal recommendations by friends; one in two reads fiction reviews in newspapers; 20 per cent find television helpful in choosing novels; and 13 per cent find radio helpful. [25] More effort is being made to link books with films and television - with vivid effects on book buyers and library users. One who asked for a copy of *Room with a View* would only be content with the version that had a scene from the film on the cover!

Some libraries get very many requests from readers, 'things they see in the Sunday papers . . . it's usually stuff we buy anyway,' said an Inner London librarian. Different branches have different readerships. 'On Monday morning the regulars come in with up to six or eight requests for books reviewed in the Sunday papers,' said another Londoner, reminiscing about 'Swiss Cottage readers'. A Yorkshire librarian noted that

> 'some people don't bother to go to the shelves, they use only requests - older readers, the sort who would have sent in their lists to the subscription library - they ask for non-fiction, coffee-table books, books on houses and gardens, that sort of thing . . . We usually order everything requested by the readers, unless it's something very expensive, or a subject of very restricted interest; those we can get from other libraries for them.'

No one was prepared to hazard a guess on how much of a contribution readers' requests make to the book-selection process in public libraries, but there was general agreement that book reviews do influence library book-buying in this way: 'reviews are useful mostly through readers seeing them.' The other main influence is through librarians' personal reading of newspapers and magazines. Only rarely is there time at work to pursue the reviews, this mainly for selection of specialised material.

Margaret Cooter

❝(role of the reviewer is) partly to sort current literature, partly to adver_ tise the author, partly to inform the public.❞

Virginia Woolf

9. *Authors*

'I never read a book before reviewing it. It prejudices a man so.'

(Rev. Sydney Smith, 1771-1845)

Sandwiched somewhere between the publishers and the booksellers, the literary editors and the reviewers, lurk the authors. I talked with a few and asked them how they felt about being the essential filling in a sort of double-decker sandwich. Did the large hunks of bread on either side of them complement their flavour? Or did they feel swamped and misrepresented by the literary establishment? Had they been stereotyped by the critics? Did male and female reviewers treat them differently? Were they in the habit of moping for days over an acidic paragraph in *The Times Literary Supplement*? Or, did anxious friends call them on the phone, only to find each author laughing herself 'silly', as Barbara Burford sometimes does when confronted with a bad review?

I spoke with four authors whose writings encompass a variety of literary genres, including feminist polemic, historical novels, whodunnits, biographies, domestic novels, short stories and poetry. Not surprisingly, I received four completely different impressions of how it feels to be reviewed. The only point on which the authors concurred was that, whatever the individual prejudices of the men and women who reviewed their work, all - well, almost all - had read the books first. So times have clearly changed for the better!

■ Margaret Forster ■

Margaret Forster, prolific writer and author of *Georgy Girl*, *Mother*

Can You Hear Me and *Significant Sisters*, announced that her attitude towards reviews was 'probably a healthy one: I'm not paranoid, as a great many writers, especially women writers, seem to be.' She saw no differences in the way men and women have reviewed her.

Forster did admit to feelings of annoyance at the 'four novelists in 800 words syndrome', but thought that the stature of the writers, not their sex, was to answer for this kind of compressed reviewing. 'Middle-ranking people' who fall between being bestsellers and big literary names find themselves being 'squashed'; and sometimes not-so-middle-ranking writers receive the same brief coverage. Margaret Forster once wrote to the *Guardian* lamenting the fact that five novels - including one by Margaret Drabble and one by John Fowles - had been reviewed in a mere 850 words!

Being a reviewer herself, Forster can see both sides of the coin. She announced that 'It's absolute hell reviewing my kind of novel.' She believes that her books, which are concerned with the minutiae of people's domestic lives, do not lend themselves to criticism, partly because of the lack of narrative interest. According to her, this has always been a problem - even with the 'greats' in the domestic field, such as Jane Austen, whose novels are far harder to review than the swashbuckling, action-packed works of Tolstoy or Dickens.

In Forster's opinion, 'women's novels' which lend themselves to in-depth reviewing are either those in which the novelist 'is beginning almost by luck a new type of women's novel' or where the novelist has a particularly identifiable voice. Margaret Drabble is an example of a novelist who started off a genre. She was the first of what came to be called 'the graduate wife school', and people were eager to read about the sixties phenomenon of graduate wives who were combining careers and children in an innovatory way. Fay Weldon, on the other hand, is a novelist with 'a highly individual voice - idiomatic and staccato - inimitably Fay.' Forster saw herself as falling outside both these categories of novelist and therefore not attracting lengthy reviews for her fiction.

Georgy Girl, published in 1965, was the first of Margaret Forster's novels to gain widespread publicity. The fact that it was made into such a popular film led Forster to fear that she might be branded a purely 'popular' novelist. As soon as she started to write non-fiction, however, her literary standing increased. As reviewers started to take her seriously, her fiction was given more careful consideration. Forster thinks that the literary establishment becomes confused at the sight of a literary 'all-rounder'. 'It's almost as if you've proved that you can play classical music and ... pop-music.'

Nor were these the only strings to Forster's bow. In 1984, her book *Significant Sisters: The Grassroots of Active Feminism 1839-1939* was published by Martin Secker & Warburg Ltd. It comprised historical biographies of eight dynamic women, including legal campaigner Caroline Norton, first female doctor Elizabeth Blackwell, Florence Nightingale, and Josephine Butler, who campaigned against the Contagious Diseases Acts. Suddenly Forster found herself entering the arena of 'feminist writing' - and noticed that her reviews were significantly shorter than they had been for her 'straight biographies' of Bonnie Prince Charlie and William Makepeace Thackeray. She also observed that *Significant Sisters* was sent out to female reviewers, although she would have considered it more appropriate material for historians of either sex. But the book had been labelled 'feminist history', which, according to Forster, does not rate as highly in the eyes of literary editors as either 'straight biography' or the controversial feminist polemic of a Betty Friedan or a Germaine Greer. She received her worst review ever from a reviewer in *City Limits*,[1] who dismissed *Significant Sisters* as a 'potboiler', implied that it had not been thoroughly researched and accused Margaret Forster of an 'inability to conceive of feminism as a movement'. Incensed by the implication that she did not know her subject, Margaret responded with a blistering letter and was astonished to see her sarcastic invective printed in a later edition of *City Limits*.

Though this review was atypical, Forster felt that feminist critics were wary of her because she seemed to be 'trampling on their patch'. Although many, including Fay Weldon, were prepared to acknowledge Forster's 'energy' and 'scholarship'[2] as an historian and a biographer, several feminist reviewers objected to *Significant Sisters* on ideological grounds. They objected to what they saw as an indiscriminate merging of the concepts of feminism and femininity. A *Times* reviewer referred sarcastically to Forster as

> 'a finish'd gentleman from top to toe.
> Scarcely a ripple of outrage - feminist or
> feminine - disturbs the calm surface.'[3]

Another female reviewer wrote,

> 'So harmless and well-bred a creature is
> Margaret Forster's feminist that you could
> safely invite her to tea at the vicarage or
> write flattering articles about her in the
> *Mail on Sunday*.'[4]

The above review was clearly referring to an intriguing article on *Significant Sisters* which appeared in *Femail on Sunday*.[5] The female reviewer was so concerned to present feminism in a non-threatening light that she bent over backwards to apply the adjectives 'beautiful' and 'gorgeous' to as many sisters as was remotely possible. Having announced at the start of the review that 'Feminism is a dirty word. It causes a ripple of shock in mixed company' (this, by the way, is 1984), she concludes with the following paean to Forster's social campaigners: 'So next time you are tempted to reject the term 'feminist', think of these eight women whose feminism was indistinguishable from their femininity.' What greater praise, after all, could any woman ask for?

Despite everything I have just said, Margaret Forster feels she has been well reviewed, especially by men. She has found favour with the arch-sexist Auberon Waugh, and she expects to be, and indeed is, reviewed in publications ranging from the *Tribune* to the *Financial Times*. She refuses to allow friends to review her books because 'the person gets in the way of the novel.' Like Zoë Fairbairns, she dislikes the 'cult of the writer' so often engendered by rampant publicity. She even went as far as to say that 'novels should just have numbers on' and should be housed 'in plain black and white wrappers'. Like Fairbairns, she does not believe that women should review the works of other women with anything less than ruthless honesty. Forster's attitude to herself as a writer has changed over the last 20 years. She now thinks of herself as a feminist (although she used not to), and she is 'less ashamed' of the type of novel she writes. She no longer heeds the sneers of authors like Anthony Burgess who scorn the domestic novel, and she now firmly believes that:

> 'What goes on in people's heads is nothing
> to be ashamed of writing about ... You can

discover worlds in them, you don't need to span continents.'

■ **Barbara Burford** ■

Barbara Burford is the author of an anthology of short stories called *The Threshing Floor*, and she is one of four black British women poets published in the poetry anthology *A Dangerous Knowing*. This anthology, which appeared in 1984, had been reviewed worldwide because it was a 'British first' and also because there is, as Burford put it, 'a current burst of interest in black women's writing and in poetry'. The response of feminist critics to Barbara Burford has been extremely positive, along the lines of Harriet Gilbert, literary editor of the *New Statesman*, who wrote of Burford's 'wise voice luring us to worlds where magic coexists with contemporary politics, wit with compassion and friendship with lush sensuality. Her vision is new, ancient, entire.' It was impossible for Burford to say whether male reviewers were prejudiced against her, for the simple (or perhaps complex) reason that, as far as she knows, no men have yet reviewed her books.

Being pigeonholed as a black writer has irked Burford at times, especially when she finds her books under the black writing sections of bookshops and not under fiction. She is also annoyed when she feels she is being 'tokenised' or reviewed merely on the grounds that she is black. But reviews from other writers are often stimulating and constructive, because they are written by people who share the same craft.

Barbara Burford is well aware that black women writers are 'the flavour of the month' as far as literary editors and reviewers are concerned. Alice Walker paved the way by winning the Pulitzer prize in 1983 for her bestselling novel *The Color Purple*. The impact created by this novel, as well as by the works of the equally esteemed Maya Angelou, has created a situation whereby new black women writers are likely to receive more reviews and publicity than new white women writers. According to Burford, 'Black men are complaining long and hard because the black male writers are almost disappearing.'

How long this trend will continue cannot be predicted, but Barbara Burford is hoping that the verbal outpourings lavished on black female writers will lead to something more enduring. She looks forward to a time when young black women can go into a library and find a whole section on black writing. She is also looking to black writers to create a literary tradition which will include all kinds of writing; not just what she describes as 'a little black pain undressed', but writing that is frivolous and funny.

> 'Young women do not want to be depressed all the time. . . When you are black and a woman, you know it. You need stuff to take you out of it.'

Barbara Burford is not going to feel happy until she sees the black equivalent of Mills and Boon established. How, I wondered, would feminist reviewers react to a stream of almost identical black romances?

■ Andrea Dworkin ■

'It isn't difficult to despise loony feminists like **Andrea** Dworkin, but I promise you that it has nothing to do with the fact that they are all physically repulsive to a man.'[6]

That promise, so casually proffered by Jeffrey Bernard in the *Spectator*, raises an interesting question. When male writers are reviewed, is similar emphasis placed on their appearance? To put it less obliquely, why is it that some reviewers seem incapable of distinguishing between the way a female author writes and the way she looks?

Andrea Dworkin, American radical feminist and author of *Pornography: Men Possessing Women*, *Right-Wing Women* and *Ice and Fire*, has suffered much at the hands of reviewers. British critics have festooned her with epithets ranging from 'Ice Maiden'[7] to 'Gob of Goo'[8] and American critics have done their best to ignore her altogether.

Dworkin's only work to attract review coverage in the United States was *Pornography*, a powerful diatribe against the ways men exploit and degrade women. The book met with a vicious response from both a 'feminist' reviewer in *The New York Times Review* and a male reviewer in the *Washington Post*. These two reviews set the tone for all the others and, far from arousing the curiosity of potential readers, frightened them away. According to Dworkin, the stigma created by such adverse publicity led to women in offices being threatened and harassed by their bosses for reading *Pornography*. She thought it 'ethically shocking' for a woman to write a damning review of another woman's work in *The New York Times*, because it meant - quite simply - that 'the writer was dead'. Dworkin explained that the literary influence of this paper exceeds that of any other publication in America; 'unless a book is reviewed by *The New York Times*, it won't even get into the bookstores.'

Andrea Dworkin's next book, *Right-Wing Women: The Politics of Domesticated Females*, was completely ignored by *The New York Times*, because it was too politically contentious. Described by Dworkin as a work which

> 'takes a serious look at why certain women
> align themselves with right-wing men and
> what is the material reality that creates
> these loyalties which are against their
> self-interest,'

it was unlikely to appeal to a male-dominated publication concerned with maintaining the status quo.

Andrea Dworkin and other feminist writers tried to challenge the attitude of *The New York Times* towards women and feminist writers. At a meeting of the Writers Guild, Dworkin and colleagues selected 'extraordinarily insulting' reviews of the works of eminent feminist writers, such as Kate Millet and Adrienne Rich. *But*, when reading these aloud to the audience, they replaced the names of the women with the names of eminent male writers. The audience was stunned by the derogatory tone of the reviews and refused to believe that they had actually been written - until it was proved otherwise. The exposure of such prejudiced reviewing of feminist writers had a dramatic effect on that occasion, but no action resulted.

Andrea and her colleagues continued with their attempts to storm *The New York Times*. They took part in organised letter-writing campaigns, hunted down a particularly sexist reviewer (only to find themselves carted away by the police) and set up the *Feminist Review of Books*. But *The New York Times* remained as obdurate as 'a military fortress'. It still had the power to destroy feminist writers in a number of ways. It could make a feminist writer 'famous', so that her privacy would be totally invaded, and

Authors

83

she would become 'a lightning rod for other people's hostility towards women and feminism'. It could also destroy by reviewing a writer contemptuously, or by not reviewing her at all.

Dworkin knows how it feels to be ostracised not only by reviewers but also by the so-called feminist publishers in America who, according to Dworkin, tend to have 'a narrow ideological point of view'. She thinks that her work 'has always fallen outside the particular fads of the women's movement in America', because of her refusal to deal with any other subject, except one: 'confronting male power'. Ironically, the American feminist publisher, Daughters, accused her of writing 'like a man' - a sentiment echoed by several British reviewers. Stanley Reynolds, in a 1982 edition of *Punch*, described her as the 'Leon Trotsky of the sex war' and went on to pay her a back-handed compliment when he stated: 'She writes with an aggressive manner, like a man. Except that no men write with such utter conviction these days.' On the whole, British reviewers have been intrigued, mesmerised and sometimes horrified by Dworkins's books, and have given her extensive coverage. *Ice and Fire*, a novel which American publishing houses all turned away, attracted a flurry of reviews when it was published by Martin Secker & Warburg Ltd in 1986. A male reviewer in the *Guardian* referred to it as a first novel which 'festers, stinks, and crackles on the page with a loathing and a striving that defies one to ignore',[9] and a reviewer in the magazine *Options* described it as, 'A feminist tract viewed with the compulsive fascination of a blackhead begging to be squeezed.'[10]

America has so far resisted the temptation to squeeze that blackhead, for fear of letting loose too explosive an influence in a conformist, right-wing climate. According to Dworkin, a number of American feminists are themselves pro-pornography; and pornographic books float in and out of publishing houses with remarkable ease, effortlessly attracting mainstream attention. Dworkin believes there is actually 'a collusion between the media in the United States and the pornographers', exemplified by media treatment of the Minneapolis hearings. At these hearings, women came forward for the first time ever to talk (to Dworkin) about their personal experiences of sexual abuse. This material was subsequently incorporated into a report, issued by the Attorney General, which found a causal relationship between pornography and sexual violence. At the time, however, Andrea and her colleague, Catherine Mackinnon, could not find a publishing house willing to publish their material on the Minneapolis hearings; and when their efforts, backed by the Attorney General's report, eventually led to the passing of a Civil Rights Law which at last defined pornography as a form of sexual discrimination against women, they were completely ignored by the mainstream press. Instead, a book opposing the new Civil Rights Law was hailed as a major publication and reviewed everywhere. When the Minneapolis hearings were eventually published, the publisher was none other than *Penthouse Magazine*, and the peculiarly qualified authors none other than the employees of *Penthouse*.

According to Dworkin, political and feminist writers in the United States face major obstacles in getting their books 'through the publishing establishment to the people', in a country whose editors act as 'thought police for the Government' and whose feminist presses are habitually blocked by distribution networks 'controlled primarily by organised crime'.

■ Zoë Fairbairns ■

Zoë Fairbairns, author of *Benefits*, *Stand We At Last* and *Here Today*, started life as a teenage novelist in the sixties, and suffered accordingly. Her first novel, *Live As Family*, published in 1968, attracted a great deal of critical attention along the lines of 'this attractive brunette' and 'bright-eyed student'. Fairbairns was annoyed to find herself promoted - in reviews and on jacket covers - as a dewy teenager with a coy smile, when she wanted her ideas to be taken seriously.

Times have changed for feminist writers, but even now Zoë Fairbairns still encounters 'bra-burning' jokes from some male reviewers and naïve descriptions of her 'not looking like a feminist', a comment which, as Fairbairns pointed out, reveals more about the reviewer than it does about the writer. Zoë Fairbairns has had plenty of experience of contradictory reviewing, where a publication has given her an unfavourable review in its literary pages and a favourable review in its feature pages. One example of this occurred in *The Sunday Times* in 1984, when Anne Boston slated *Here Today* as:

'A whodunnit set in the synthetic half-world of secretarial agencies [with] ex-temp of the year, Antonia, herpes-ridden, husbandless and ousted by word processors, turning sleuth ... Deliberately downbeat theme: dull and improbable dénouement.''

One month earlier, however, Sally Vincent had given Zoë a glowing review in the feature pages, describing her as a feminist novelist who had found 'a medium that might be described as happy.'² These two well-known reviewers clashed again when Anne Boston, then the literary editor of *Cosmopolitan*, refrained from buying serial rights for *Here Today*, and refused to review it. Sally Vincent sprang once more to the rescue in a *Cosmopolitan* feature on female role models, in which she describes the herpes-ridden and husbandless Antonia thus:

'She kicks Jane Eyre, Madame Bovary and Anna Karenina into a cocked hat along with Meg, Jo, Beth and Amy and every damn thing Katy did. She leads me to believe that if we want role models, we'll have to invent them for ourselves with only our own images and each other for assistance.''³

How can such paradoxical reviewing be explained? Perhaps Zoë Fairbairns finds favour in the feature pages because she has created heroines whose conflicts parallel those encountered by women today. These heroines can easily be adopted as role models, because they are so well-balanced, falling as they do exactly between

'the comfy conservatism where heroines seek their destiny in men's beds [and the] hard-liners [who] soldier on into the wilder shores of loneliness and lesbianism with their integrity virgo-intacta and their bellies full of lentils,'⁴ as Sally Vincent wrote in her *Sunday Times* article.

Zoë Fairbairns's worst ever review appeared in *The Times Literary Supplement*, where a male reviewer, Savkar Altinel, seemed to think that *Here Today* was an excuse for subliminal advertising of such products as the *Guardian*, *Options*, tampax and the *TLS* (spot the odd one out). He accused Fairbairns of indulging in a 'grab-life-by-the-lapels approach' and implied that the book was the invention of Zoë's publisher and her agent, whereas, in fact, it was entirely Zoë's own idea.

Zoë Fairbairns experience of reviews has changed completely since the late sixties, when her feminist ideas landed on stony ground. The growth of a feminist movement in Britain since then has meant that many women (and men) respond to her novels with what she calls 'a kind of understanding' and 'a willingness to engage with the ideas, even if they don't like the book'. For example, Jane Gardam writing in *Books and Bookmen*, understands the predicament of Antonia in a 'dangerous and desolate world' of temp secretaries who know 'they will soon be replaced by computers'; but she is also critical of *Here Today*, stating that the characters all speak 'the same awful Radio Two patois'. Fairbairns enjoys encountering informed criticism and said that reading Jane Gardam's review 'was like having a good conversation'. She does not believe that it is the duty of sisterhood for women to like each other's books. She believes that female reviewers should give honest criticism, but in a constructive way.

As far as choosing reviewers is concerned, Fairbairns is sent forms by her publisher and asked to suggest if she has friends who might be interested in reviewing her books. This gives her the chance to find a sympathetic reviewer. But 'hype' or extravagant praise are not what she is after. She dislikes 'dishonest publicity', such as the use of the word 'bestseller' about a book that has not yet been offered for sale!

Finally, Zoë Fairbairns explained how feminism has helped her as a writer:

> 'It has given validation to the things I have always believed, it has identified a readership for feminist books, and it is very stimulating to the imagination. The

Authors

clash between feminist ideas and other
ideas produces a shower of stories ...
enough to last a lifetime.'

Jane Tarlo

❝Reviewers are usually
people who would have
been poets, historians, bio-
graphers etc if they could;
they have tried their talents
at one or at the other and
have failed; therefore they
turn critics.❞

Samuel Taylor Coleridge

Conclusion

What then *is* a woman's place on the book review pages? It is apparent from our study that there is a clear distinction between what are considered to be 'general' publications and women's magazines. The latter obviously have a predominantly female readership and their choice of books and reviewers reflects this fact. However, when it comes to the so-called 'general' publications, we found that our initial observation of a bias against women mainly proved to be true - in terms of the number of female authors reviewed, the amount of space devoted to women's books and their positioning on the page.

The more specialist the publication, the more the editorial staff appeared to be aware of this imbalance on their book pages. However, they tended to justify or explain the bias in terms of the smaller number of female academics and specialists, both for writing and reviewing purposes, claiming that women were less interested in serious subjects such as politics and foreign affairs, and had less free time for the poorly paid and time-consuming work of reviewing.

The most surprising group in our survey proved to be the national newspapers. Their scores on our tables were generally low - they reviewed fewer women's books than the percentage published, gave them less prominence and shorter reviews - and yet according to their own circulation figures, their readership averages 55 per cent male and 45 per cent female. Despite their blatant discrimination against women, most of the editorial staff we talked to were supremely complacent, shrugging off our questions and claiming that there was no bias in their choice of books for review or of the reviewer.

Most publications seem uncomfortable with women's books. Books on feminism, for instance, tend to be regarded as women's interest rather than as politics, whereas a male-orientated political book is deemed to be of general interest. Literary editors are divided between those who try making an effort to link books by women authors with female reviewers and see this as a positive step, and others who attempt to break away from such stereotyping. Male reviewers sometimes appear defensive about reviewing women's books. This opening comment from a male reviewer given five books on feminism to review for the *London Review of Books* is not untypical: 'Why these books should have come to a male reviewer is perhaps more a question for the editor than myself.'[1] Hardly a question that a female reviewer given a political book to review would ask. Then there are the remarks directed at women's appearance and sexual attraction which are never seen in a review of a book written by a man.

There is also a tendency on the general publications to ghettoise women's writing, relegating it to composite reviews at the bottom of the page under a heading 'Women Writers', or even worse, to the women's page, where it tends to become a book notice rather than a review - a typical example of this is the *Guardian*. In such cases, the literary editor may say, 'We review lots of books by women'; but this complacent attitude does not take into account the smaller amount of space devoted to women writers on their pages. What would be their reaction to a suggestion that the books page should cover women authors in depth with men's books grouped together at the bottom?

Since publications which define their market as primarily women favour reviews of books by women and use female reviewers, publishers are inclined to target their review copies of books by women at women's magazines, where they know they are more likely to obtain coverage. Consequently, they tend to concentrate less on the general publications, newspapers and Sunday supplements. In other words, books by women authors are categorised as 'women's interest'. This definition is arbitrary - it is certainly not that of the author or of the reader. Books by men, on the other hand, are deemed to be of general interest - hence their domination of the book review pages aimed at a general market.

Why all the fuss, people may ask. Women's books are getting reviewed, so why worry about whether it is by the women's magazines or by the general publications. In fact, some people might argue that women authors get a better deal precisely because they are virtually guaranteed coverage by a certain category of magazine. The concern arises because women's magazines, like women authors, are not regarded seriously by the book trade, or the literary world. A review from *Good Housekeeping* would be unlikely to be used as a selling point for the book, unless it was obviously aimed only at a female readership, whereas a review from *The Times Literary Supplement* or the *Observer* will be cited in the publicity blurb and on paperback jackets. In addition, it is the reviews in the mass-circulation Sunday papers and supplements which are the most apt to influence sales - this is endorsed by publishers, booksellers and libraries. The publishers, in particular, state that while any review helps, it is the Sundays and the supplements which sell large numbers of books.

This being the case, the fact that it is the most influential publications which show the most bias is an obvious cause for concern. It is vital that women authors receive more review coverage in the general publications, and yet they seem trapped in a vicious circle: publications which feature fewer reviews of books by women are sent fewer books by women to review. They receive fewer books by women, therefore they review fewer books by women. Can this circle be broken?

Literary editors may claim that their pages reflect society, but people in positions of responsibility who deal with the world of ideas are the best placed to influence changes in attitudes. In producing pages biased against women, they are perpetuating existing prejudice and subtly shaping people's perceptions of reality.

Practically, what can be done? We hope that this survey, which for the first time provides comprehensive facts and figures bearing out our initial observations as readers of the book review pages, will provide publishers, literary editors and readers with some food for thought and provide a climate for change. Change can only occur if there is an awareness of the need for change.

On an individual level, those of us who work in the book trade, especially in publishing, can attempt to change attitudes in publicity departments responsible for sending out review copies. Those of us who are readers and consumers can write letters of complaint to publications every time we see too few women's books being reviewed or unjust reviewing in terms of position, length or tone. More women could step forward and offer to write reviews and suggest books for review. One literary editor, conscious of the problem, stressed how hard it was to actually find women reviewers, especially for the more traditional male preserves of specialist and academic books. So it is up to women too to make an effort in these areas. And the more women reviewers there are, the more will be encouraged to come forward.

Although it is partly up to women to realise that we can play a more prominent role on the book pages, it is particularly up to literary editors to make a conscious effort to include more women reviewers and more reviews of women's books. It is not enough to say we want to see more women literary editors. That in itself does not guarantee equality on the book review pages. Women isolated in positions of power are often forced to espouse male values to keep their position (the Maggie Thatcher syndrome), so although we would like to see more women literary editors, they need the support of their readership and staff in endorsing a policy of balance on the review pages. Until this happens, women's voices will continue to be stifled.

Notes

Introduction

1. James Craigie Robertson, *Quarterly Review*, Vol. 108, July-October 1860.
2. Auberon Waugh, *Daily Mail*, 19 November 1981.

■ **Part One** ■

Methodology

1. For analytical reasons, the December 1985 issue of *Woman and Home* was excluded from the survey.

The Literary Dinner Party

1. The 20 per cent figure is mentioned by Lynne Spender in her article 'The politics of publishing: selection and rejection of women's words in print' appearing in *Women's Studies International Forum*, Vol. 6, No. 5. On page 472 she says: 'Even so, publishers seem to have an unspoken (at least in public) agreement that published books written by women should remain at approximately 20 per cent of the number of published books written by men.' This is also referred to by Dale Spender in her unpublished paper 'A difference of view: reviewing male reviewers', presented

at Cambridge University in April 1984. All our attempts to find statistics offering a breakdown by sex of author for published books in Britain were unsuccessful.

2. The sample size was based on the 'worst possible case', where 50 per cent of books would be written by women, at a confidence level of 95 per cent, and required a minimum of 385 titles. Of the 652 tabulated, 410 were general and 242 specialised.

3. This calculation involves taking the mean of the lengths of reviews for male and female authors, dividing each by the overall total mean and then finding the difference between the resulting proportions. This produces a gauge of how much a publication did or did not comparatively favour women in the space allotted to reviews. While the results are roughly in line with our findings of favouritism based on percentages, those figures were based on data pertaining only to the favourite sex of author. The results of this calculation, however, take directly into account how a publication treated both sexes and so differ slightly in some ways. Here then are the full results, starting from those favouring women most (positive numbers denote a publication that favours women while negative figures mean it did not): *Company* .45; *New Socialist* .24; *Woman and Home* .23; *Cosmopolitan* .18; *City Limits* .17; *Good Housekeeping* .11; *Punch* .10; *New Statesman* .05; *She* .05; *Observer* .04; *School Librarian* .02; *Literary Review* .02; *The Times Higher Education Supplement* -.14; *Spectator* -.10; *Fiction Magazine* -.13; *Financial Times* -.14; *The Times Literary Supplement* -.16; *London Review of Books* -.18; *Spare Rib* -.18; *Daily Telegraph* -.28; *Sunday Times* -.25; *Guardian* -.27; *New Society* -.29; *Mail on Sunday* -.34; *Marxism Today* -.35; *Options* -.37; *The Times* -.45; and *Listener* -.51.

Fact and Fiction

1. Again, *Spare Rib* also showed this bias, but the result is skewed by the fact only one men's book was reviewed over the year and it was non-fiction.

2. *Spare Rib* technically belongs on this list, but was excluded because its inclusion hinged on just one review of a man's book which is not necessarily indicative.

■ Part Two ■

Literary Editors

Quotations are taken from letters and conversations with literary editors or with staff on the book pages.

1. J.D. Hendry, 'The administrative role of the book-review editor', *Reviews and Reviewing: A Guide,* ed. A.J. Walford, London, Mansell, 1986.
2. Ibid.
3. Gaby Weiner, *Guardian*, 25 January 1986.
4. Dale Spender, *Women of Ideas*, London, Arc, 1983.

Libraries

Unattributed quotations are taken from interviews with librarians.

1. 'Public library spending has fallen by 34.2 per cent in real terms since 1978/9 . . . annual book additions have declined by 1.3 million since 1978. . . eighteen local authorities have cut more than half their book fund. . . books which would previously have been withdrawn after four years had to remain on the shelves for nearly ten years.. . (in some libraries) books were being selected solely on the basis of price, with whole subject areas being abandoned.' 'Public library spending falls by one third in six years', *Bookseller*, 7 November 1986, p.1860.
2. Andy Stephens, 'The British National Bibliography - aims and uses', *Bookseller*, 31 October 1986, pp.1780-84 (p.1781).
3. A.J. Walford, 'The art of reviewing' in his *Reviews and Reviewing: A Guide.* London, Mansell, 1986, p.7.
4. David Spiller, *Book Selection: An Introduction to Principles and Practice*, 4th edition, London, Clive Bingley, 1984, p.78.
5. Tom Martin, 'The process of book selection', *Bookseller*, 17 October 1986, pp.1590-95.
6. Judith Serebnik, 'An analysis of publishers of books reviewed in key library journals', *Library and Information Science Research*, Vol.6, No.3, 1984, pp.298-303. Favourable reviews outnumber unfavourable reviews, 3-to-1 (*Encyclopedia of Library and Information*

Science, New York, Dekker, 1978; Vol.25, p.318).

7.	Thanks to the librarians in London, Manchester and Kirklees who took time to answer questions and add their comments. Thanks also to those Women in Libraries who responded to a postal questionnaire.

8.	Spiller, pp. 153-4.

9.	R.W. Trueswell, 'Some behavioral patterns of library users: the 80/20 rule', *Wilson Library Bulletin*, Vol.43, No.5, 1969, pp.458-69.

10.	BNB Research Fund Study on Book Selection Sources. Interim report on pilot study. BLLD, Research Section, June 1978.

11.	Wages take 51 per cent of the budget, while books etc. take 18 per cent (CIPFA, *Public Library Statistics 1985-86 Actuals*).

12.	Barbara Jennings and Lyn Sear, 'How readers select fiction - a survey in Kent', *Public Library Journal*, Vol.1, No.4, 1986, pp.43-7.

13.	Barry Hall, 'Book selection in a public library' in *From Publisher to Reader*, London, Library Association, 1972.

14.	Based on figures that 1/3 hold a valid ticket (B. Totterdell and J. Birch, *The Effective Library*, London, Library Association, 1976, p.194). 33 per cent of the population have used the library within the last year (Runcorn Distict, *Library Market Research Study*, 1978, p.25).

15.	Spiller, p.158.

16.	Jennings and Sear, p.46.

17.	In the days of the commercial circulating libraries a review in the Sunday papers would lead to instant demand - and 'the majority of new titles were dismally dead and indecently buried within three or four weeks' (Sir Robert Lusty, 'Knowing the market: the reflections of a publisher' in *Selection at Work*, ed. Frank Baguley, London, Library Association, 1978).

18.	Tameside Libraries, *Book Selection Statement*, 1982.

19.	W.H.S. Whitehouse, 'Book selection from the point of view of the library supplier' in *From Publisher to Reader*, London, Library Association, 1972, p.200.

20.	Spiller, p.178.

21.	Tameside Libraries, 1982.

22.	David Spiller, 'The provision of fiction for public libraries' *Journal of Librarianship*, Vol.12, No.4, 1980, pp.238-66.

23.	Spiller, 1984, pp.155-6.

24.	Spiller recommends that libraries display reviews of new fiction. The Kent library produces an in-house booklet of librarians' reviews of current novels - but the books need to be available, i.e. on the shelves.

25. See Spiller, 1980.

Authors

1. Deborah Philips, *City Limits*, 5 October 1984.
2. Fay Weldon, *Hampstead and Highgate Express*, 5 October 1984.
3. Gay Firth, *The Times*, 20 September 1984.
4. Joan Smith, *New Statesman*, 19 October 1984.
5. Lesley Garner, *Femail on Sunday*, 9 September 1984.
6. Jeffrey Bernard, *Spectator*, 31 January 1987.
7. Kathy Acker, *Time Out*, 9 April 1986.
8. Margaret Forster, *Literary Review*, April 1986.
9. Christopher Wordsworth, *Guardian*, 24 April 1986.
10. Aisling Foster, *Options*, April 1986.
11. Anne Boston, *The Sunday Times*, 27 May 1984.
12. Sally Vincent, *The Sunday Times*, 1 April 1984.
13. Sally Vincent, *Cosmopolitan*, February 1985.
14. Sally Vincent, *The Sunday Times*, 1 April 1984.

Conclusion

1. Christopher Norris, *London Review of Books*, 4 April 1985.

Further Reading

Blond, Anthony *The Book Book*. London, Cape, 1985.
An entertaining survey of the book trade and how publishers operate. 'Reviews', pp.136-43.

Book Review Digest, New York, H.W. Wilson, 1905-.
An American service which gathers excerpts of reviews from various sources. Ten issues a year.

Book Reviewing, ed. Sylvia E. Kamerman, Boston, Mass., The Writer, 1978.
A guide to writing book reviews for newspapers, magazines, radio and television, by leading book editors, critics and reviewers.

Drewry, John *Writing Book Reviews*, Boston, Mass., The Writer, 1966.
Step-by-step guidance on how to evaluate books in various fields (fiction, history, biography, etc.). 'The book page', pp.163-70, may be read with historical hindsight.

From Publisher to Reader. Library Association, 1972.
A publisher, a library supplier, a librarian, a bookseller give their views on the supply of books to the reading public.

'Impulse buying of books', London, Publishers Association, July 1982.
A survey of how many books are bought on impulse and what generated the impulse.

Noble, D.H. and C.N. *A Survey of Book Reviews, Oct-Dec 1973*, London, Noble & Beck, 1974.
An analysis of nearly 4,000 book reviews which appeared on the regular book pages of 12 national daily and Sunday newspapers.

Reviewing the Reviews: A Guide, ed. A.J. Walford, London, Mansell, 1986.
>Starts with a survey of reviewing in general, and the editor's role; goes on to give details of reviewing sources in academic subject areas.

Spender, Dale 'A difference of view: reviewing male reviewers' (unpublished: paper presented at Cambridge University, 26 April 1984).
>Includes 'some interesting figures' on books, reviews and surveys.

Spender, Lynne *Intruders on the Rights of Men: Women's Unpublished Heritage*, London, Pandora, 1983.

----- 'The politics of publishing: selection and rejection of women's words in print', *Women's Studies International Quarterly*, Vol. 6, No. 5, 1983, pp.469-73.
>Evaluation of a book in the initial stages of its publishing history.

Spiller, David *Book Selection: An Introduction to Principles and Practice*, 4th edition, London, Clive Bingley, 1984.
>The processes involved in making stock available in the library. Chapter 5, 'Book evaluation', pp.65-81.

Sutherland, J.A. *Fiction and the Fiction Industry*, Athlone Press, 1978.
>Chapter 5, 'The reviewing establishment', pp.84-106.

Tunstall, Jeremy *The Media in Britain*, London, Constable, 1983.
>Puts newspapers, magazines and their audiences into social and historical context. A good starting point for looking at the industry's policies and control.

White, Cynthia L. *The Women's Periodical Press in Briain, 1946-1976*, HMSO, 1977.
>One of the working papers of the Royal Commission on the Press. Historical background; content analysis by type of women's periodical.

Whittaker, Kenneth *Systematic Evaluation: Methods and Sources for Assessing Books*, London, Clive Bingley, 1982.
>New books; book reviews; reviewing journals; locating reviews - pp.105-22.

Further reading

99

Women's Review of Books, Wellesley, Mass., The Wellesley College
Centre for Research on Women, 1983-.
In format similar to *New York Times Review of Books*.

Woolf, Virginia *Reviewing*, London, Hogarth Press, 1939.
Concentrates on the reviewing of poetry, drama and fiction, and on
'the value of the reviewer's office'. A note by Leonard Woolf
distinguishes between reviewing and literary criticism.

For further information about Women in Publishing, send s.a.e to:
Women in Publishing,
c/o J. Whitaker Ltd,
12 Dyott St,
London WC1A 1DF

Appendix: Survey Form

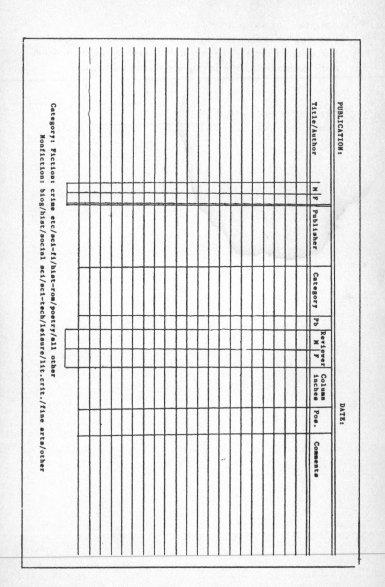

PUBLICATION:									DATE:
Title/Author	M	F	Publisher	Category	Pb	Reviewer M	F	Column inches	Pos.	Comments

Category: Fiction: crime etc/sci-fi/hist-rom/poetry/all other
Nonfiction: biog/hist/social sci/sci-tech/leisure/lit.crit./fine arts/other

Index